*The thoughts, opinions, beliefs and ideas expressed
in this book are the authors.
(Master Percy Twenty-Five Brown)*

MILLION MAN MARCH
BOOK OF THE AMERICAN DEAD

PERCY TWENTY-FIVE BROWN

Copyright © 2024 by Percy Twenty-Five Brown.

ISBN: 979-8-89465-026-5 (sc)
ISBN: 979-8-89465-064-7 (hb)
ISBN: 979-8-89465-027-2 (e)

All rights reserved. No part of this publication may be reproduced, distributed, or transmitted in any form or by any means, including photocopying, recording, or other electronic or mechanical methods, without the prior written permission of the author, except in the case of brief quotations embodied in critical reviews and certain other noncommercial uses permitted by copyright law.

Printed in the United States of America.

Integrity Publishing
39343 Harbor Hills Blvd Lady Lake,
FL 32159

www.integrity-publishing.com

To Ruby – The love of my life

CONTENTS

Chapter 1: Old Man 1

Chapter 2: Hell 18

Chapter 3: The last great African American hero. 33

Chapter 4: The Backside of the Bell Curve 58

Chapter 5: The Secret of the N-word. .76

Chapter 6: An Indigenous Man's Prayer 85

Chapter 7: Atonement. 94

Chapter 8: GOD first 104

CHAPTER 1

Old Man

"Right over there is where Snoop Dogg shot that guy, I was here when it happened," Mike said, pointing to an area of few feet away from where we were standing.

"I don't know man… I used to think that becoming rich and famous was the way out of this mess. It looks like there's no way out. Gang life is the only thing for us. The gang is the only place we can find love."

"I heard about Snoop Dogg being involved in his shooting," I said. "I didn't know this was the park. I bring my little girl to play here often. I didn't know things like that happened around here."

"You'd be surprised. Just a few weeks ago a girl got shot as she stood waiting for a bus right down in Venice. She was shot just because she was black. I know you heard about the war between the black and Mexican gangs?"

"You guys don't understand that divide and conquer thing, that's what they run on you. Slavery made a lot of Americans rich. They miss it now and would like to get back to it. I remember when there was segregation. Black people knew what was going on because whites did not try to hide the hatred. It was the same during segregation and Jim Crow, that's what was going on when I was born.

I was around seven years old when Ms. Rosa Parks refused to give up her seat on the bus for a white man. I remember the bus boycotts. I remember mass meetings that were sometimes held at my grandmother's home. Black people would get together to try to find ways they could help each other get to work. We pretty much had to stick together then. We had no choice.

We marched for equal rights, but we never got equal rights. We got something they called "integration" which was the worst thing that could have happened. Sure, we could go into white restaurants and other businesses. We could even move into white neighborhoods, but there was a lot less togetherness. Some black people thought they could escape being black.

Affirmative action helped us to get some decent jobs with decent pay, but they are now ready to take that back. It was around 1965 when we got the right to vote. Reagan signed an amendment in the 80s to extend this right for 25 years. Now white America is trying hard to make guys that look like you and I did not deserve these rights in the first place so they can convince people they should take them back."

"No, it's all about the drug money. See, Mexicans think blacks are too aggressive when they deal drugs. They fight over territory and a lot of other stupid little things. At one time there were drive by shootings every day."

Mike pulled out a fresh cigarette and lit it from the one he was smoking. He took a drink from a 40 oz beer, wiped his mouth then continued. "I have been gangbanging a long time. We must throw down sometimes, we have to do drive-byes sometimes, but just to shoot innocent people walking down the street... I don't know, it seems cowardly to me."

I was amazed that a gang member would consider it cowardly to do a drive by shooting when gang members were thought to be responsible for most of them. I knew from the experience that I had

had as a gang member, a lot of things you hear in the news about gangs are not true. However, before this conversation I had never had anything to say to the new generation of gang members.

I had escaped gang life. I was a Marine Corps veteran and had gotten the chance to go to school. I now considered myself an intelligent law-abiding citizen and gang members were people to be always avoided. Having been involved in the gang life myself, I knew how dangerous these young men could be. My mind drifted for a moment. A few months before, I had experienced another conversation with another young man who had upset me to the point where I never completely recovered.

This young man had encountered an incident so disturbing that it had caused him mental damage. I had encountered the same situation nearly 30 years before. I met the man briefly at the Veteran's Administration hospital. We had a few minutes to talk before the orderly came to take him away. He was desperate for answers as to what was happening to him.

It was as if fate had set it up for me to be there at that time. I could have explained a few things to the man from my previous experiences, but I didn't. All I did was listen to his story and think about myself in the same situation. There was no help for me, and I didn't think there would be any help for him either. My position was, if God is on your side, you will survive. If not, there's no hope anyway.

I did not know this man and I felt like I had nothing to do with what was happening to him. I had learned over the years to tend to my own business. I was satisfied that most of the people who knew me considered me to be a Vietnam era veteran who was slightly crazy. A lot of Marines are considered crazy. I was alone, and I very seldom spoke to people I did not know. I could not explain the guilt I felt by not saying anything to this man. It was like I had met myself 20 years in the past.

I kind of felt like this conversation with Mike was a chance to redeem myself. Once again, I found myself talking to a young man who could have been me 30 years ago. He was a gang member the same as I had been at his age, not because he or I wanted to be. That was the life we grew up in. He was desperate for a way out, the same as I had been at his age. Nothing seemed to work for us.

We were both raised without fathers, and life was full of unanswered questions. We grew up anxious to learn to become men, but there are no role models for fatherless black American males. It was not often that you ran into an older man who could give advice. However, occasionally, you run into an old man who had amassed a great amount of wisdom. A person who could tell you something that could help you understand more about the strange world we found ourselves in, if you were willing to listen, sometimes, that person appeared.

Growing up, I always look to older, wiser men for advice. I found out that you must first be able to respect the man before you're willing to take his advice. If you live to be 100 years old, you're lucky if you meet any man worthy of respect. If you are so-called African American, you may find, that those referred to as black leaders are the ones you can trust the least.

In segregated communities, just hanging out together as we grew up caused us to be called "gangs." Older black men who were employed considered themselves to be "role models." They encouraged some youth to avoid the gangs. They were not wrong, we did get into trouble, but it was mostly because sometimes, we did not know the right things to do.

With our black men with jobs working their butts off sometimes for salaries like $0.50 an hour. We considered them to be slaves and we did not want to be like them. Contrary to what some white people believe, we certainly did not want to be like white people. We were of a mindset that, no human being who could come up with slavery, Jim Crow, lynchings, and segregation could convince anyone that they were good people. Even the ones who tried to convince us that they were nice, went too far out of their way to convince us that we were inferior and cursed by God.

Mike was with some other gang members when I met him. There were at least eight of them seated on top or standing around a picnic table in the park. They all smoked cigarettes, and they all had these 40 oz beers. When I walked into the park with my 5-year-old niece, Mary, one of the young men pointed me out and they began to laugh at my long hair.

Mary gave me a kiss on the cheek and ran off to the swings. I walk towards the tree, just a few feet from where the gang members had congregated. I worked out there two or three times a week, doing Tae Kwon Do exercises. I could hear a lot of teasing from some of the young men however, I never acknowledged them.

"Hey, look man, look at this guy with the Michael Jackson hair." One of the men said. The others began to laugh.

"Hey brother man, it's the 90s. Niggers get haircuts." The teasing continued as I began stretching and warming up. When I began practicing punches and kicks, it became apparent that I had all their attention.

"Go over there and tell that that nigger that, that ain't shit. I can show him how to fight." One of them said.

"This guy looks like he's pretty good, you might get your ass kicked." "Bull shit! Can't no old man kick my ass." "OK, I'll go over there and tell him you want to challenge him."

By this time, I had completed practicing the forms and began doing kicks and punches on one of the trees that I had used as a punching bag. Each one of men were amazed to see someone punching a tree. I believe that it was at this point they started to develop respect. Even in this high-tech society, men still consider physical strength one of God's greatest gifts. When asked, young men say the same thing today that they said when I was growing up. "The only men I respect, are men who can fight better than me."

There was silence after the shock the young men experienced seeing me punching and kicking the tree. That conversation continued.

"Did you see that nigger punch that tree?"

"Damn! His hands and feet must be as hard as rocks."

"You can tell he's got experience. He's probably one of them OGs (Original Gangsters)."

"Yeah, he must have been one of them regulators."

"You still want me to tell him you want to fight him?"

"You can tell him whatever the fuck you want to tell him."

"OK, I'm going over there right now and tell him you'll fight him."

"You just go right ahead. If he comes over here, I'm going to tell him that I didn't say shit."

There was laughter, then a police car drove by, slowed to watch the men around the bench, then drove off. When the police car finally got out of sight, the young men knew that the car would return and the next time they would be harassed. They all left the park; all except Mike. I was still practicing when I heard him call me. I looked around at the lone gang member left on the bench.

"Were you talking to me man?" I asked politely. "You know that shit is for real these days."

"I don't understand. What shit?"

"That Karate shit. You know people kill for real these days."

"It was for real when I was your age too. The only difference between your generation and mine is that you guys shoot each other. In my day you had to know how to fight. When we had a disagreement, we met in the park at night or on the railroad tracks or in alleys. We went at it hand to hand, knuckle to knuckle. Some guys would carry knives, clubs, or chains, but it was still a fair fight.

For us the only ones who use guns were cowards or what we call the 'hard-core gangsters', who did armed robberies and were ready to shoot it out with the police. One thing we all agreed on was, men depend on God, cowards depend on weapons."

Mike took a drink from his 40 oz, lit up another cigarette, and introduced himself. He showed me where Snoop Dogg had allegedly shot someone. Then we compared the way young black men grew up during the 50s and 60s with the way they grow up today.

"It's not that drive by shootings 'seem' cowardly," I said. "They 'are' cowardly acts. However, we live in a society that will never give up the gun because those in power realize that none of their power will exist without the gun. If you study history, you'll find that the invention of the gun was the start of the weak being able to control the strong. Since this is against the laws of nature, nature will eventually destroy everything that has been built because of this evil. Do you think the Indians would have lost their land if they had the same weapons the whites had?"

"That was different. The Indians were uncivilized."

"You don't know anything about Indians or what the word civilized means. You're just programmed to look at them as being different. When we were kids, we used to joke about the Indians too. When I grew up, I found out that this government has done more to mislead people about minorities than most would believe. Indians didn't have the weapons to defend themselves, but even if they had, they were not prepared for the most dangerous and destructive weapon of all – The LIE. Tribal people believed in gods. They would not offend the gods or risk their own destruction by using lies. Their mistake was in thinking other men were honest."

"All I ever heard about the Indians was that they had too many superstitions, like they wouldn't fight on holy ground, they wouldn't fight at certain times of day and night and stuff like that."

"Indians had their beliefs, but mainly the laws of their land were more from being outgunned and to trusting. Did you know that millions of Indians were wiped out by the government giving them free blankets infected with smallpox?"

"Didn't the government know that they were infected? The blankets, I mean."

"Hell yes! They knew. That was the plan. Did you hear about the black men in Tuskegee Alabama who were experimented on with syphilis?"

"What!?"

"Yeah, I've heard two different stories. In Alabama, I was told that black men would go to the doctors for something like the flu. The doctors would give them shots and infect them with syphilis; then would be monitoring them to see how the disease was progressing. I've heard white doctors in the media say that only the ones already infected were experimented on, but either way, it would take a serious fool to trust a doctor in this culture."

"What about black doctors?"

"Every person who is called a "Minority" in this culture has no choice but to go along with the program of "White Supremacy." Otherwise, they are imprisoned, killed, or prevented from making a decent living.

This takes us back to the Indians. A lot of Indians cannot adjust to this culture. Many died, the rest live on what they call "Reservations." Reservations is another word for prison camps. If you look back on what happened to the Indians, we can get some idea of what the plan is for us. You see, while we are fighting each other and the Latinos, people are hard at work trying to come up with some disease to wipe out everyone who is not white.

"That is where "AIDS" comes from. If you go into a bookstore, I bet you can find at least ten books about authors who have published documents allegedly proving that the United States government hired scientists to develop the AIDS virus. They were then, and are now, looking for some disease to wipe out the black population."

"What about God though? It looks like God would stop some of this stuff."

"Do you believe in God?"

"Yeah, I got deep into religion at one time. I stopped gangbanging, started to go to church. I really got into the religion thing, I went to the altar, and I got saved, even started speaking in tongues. I was happy for a while, but nothing significant happened. Then after a while, church got boring, and I found that I got more love from my brothers in the gangs than I did in church. I just got out of jail about a week ago. Man, you should have seen all the love my brothers gave me when I first got locked down."

I smiled to think about how similar our lives were. "I was into that church thing once myself. I first got involved in the Catholic religion because most of my mother's family were Catholic. And the Catholic school, I found some of the nuns to be just as evil, mean and racist as the rest. They scared me, so I started going to the Baptist Church with my grandmother. Baptist preachers were involved in so many things they were telling us "not to do", I didn't believe they really believed what they were preaching."

"That's the way I was starting to feel, Christians may not do what gangsters do but most of them do something they don't want others to know about."

"And the minorities should naturally have suspicious about the Christian religion. Most black people in this country today are Christians because they are the children of slaves who would have been killed had they not accepted the Christian religion I was surprised when I found out the same thing about Latinos."

"I still think God, I mean the True God, would step in and change things. There must be an answer."

"We do not know God. When most African Americans pray, they pray to a "god" they learn about from people who enslaved them. The black man has walked the earth thousands and thousands of years under the protection of our God. When the whites came, showing us all these machines and weapons telling us that they were from the one true God, we forgot the Gods who had protected us for all those years and followed the white man. We have been suffering and dying ever since.

Black Christians today repeat words that were beaten into them by slave masters. Black people pray and pray but nothing ever improves. You look up, the white man still has his foot on your neck. Since the coming of the white man prayers of thanks and joy have turned into prayers for salvation. The one thing we fail to realize is, our god's never left us; we left them."

"Why would anybody lie about God?"

"Everyone has their own God. The people who enslaved us, wanted to be gods themselves. They knew that all tribal people believed in some God, but since no one could really prove there was a God, they invented one to suit their needs: material wealth and the feeling of having power over the earth and its inhabitants. They did extensive studies in psychology. It was found that it did not matter whether the tribal people could prove that their Gods existed. If we believe and obey the commandments given to us, we cannot be dominated. They had to come up with ways to make us leave our God, and they did."

"Damn how come I never heard these things before?"

"Oh, I go to school whenever I can. When I can't, I find books to educate myself as much as I can."

"That's what I want to do. I want to go to school and learn about these things. I want to learn history. But not that white history, you know. I want to learn black history."

"Blacks get lured in black history. However, to get a true understanding of how we got to where we are, you need to understand the mindset of the ones who captured us. The accomplishments of slaves benefit only the slave masters. Nothing we do means anything until our freedom and our lands are restored." "What about them brothers who go to school to become lawyers, doctors and businessmen? Don't they get out of this mess?"

"One of the main things that I have learned was, there's a big difference between going to school to get an education and going to school to get a profession. I never thought I'd get a chance to go to college. When I did my only thought was how much money I can make. While I was studying computer science, I became interested in anthropology, psychology, history, art and other things.

Culture is the most important thing to learn about. Experiments were done with the Indians. Some whites believed that, if you remove an Indian completely away from his culture, cut his hair and put shoes on his feet, he'd become a white man. Meaning, he would adopt the white culture."

I was surprised that I had held Mike's attention for so long a time. He was obviously paying close attention to every word, just like I used to do when the old men used to tell me things. It brought a smile to my face to realize that I was now the old man.

The police car cruised by again. I looked around for little Mary thinking she might be ready to leave. She was running in my direction. I asked her if she was ready to go. She said "no". She gave me a big hug and kiss then ran back to the swings.

"She's a cute little girl," Mike said. "I'll bet you teach her well."

"I try to answer every question she asks."

"Back to this culture thing. How can removing people from their culture change them?"

"Over the years, people develop lifestyles that they become comfortable with. Customs and habits become a culture. All tribal people lived as they felt God wanted them to live. Being forced away from your culture is the same as being forced away from your God. It took the deaths of millions and millions of Indians and blacks to program us to be the way we are today."

"What do you mean by program?"

"I have a degree in computer science and a certificate in computer programming. When I learned about programming computers, along with psychology, I began to see how people could be programmed. That's why I have long hair. That is why I had to devote most of my time to try to find our Gods, the ones that we left. Here, you and your children are forced to go to school. The teachers' main concern is to get you to act and respond in a certain way when faced with certain situations. Truth is not important; the right response is.

The statement,' Columbus discovered America' would more than likely be marked correct on a test. However, if you examine what is being implied and why, you'd see that statements like these serve more to hide the truth. A student's main concern is being able to give the proper response if he or she plans to pass the course. This is programming."

"But what if a student realizes that he's being taught a bunch of crap, he might have put the right response on the test, but he would know better."

"It's not important whether you know the truth. The purpose of programming is to get you to act or respond in a certain way. If you feel that you are in a position where you find it better to do as you're told, rather than do what you feel is right, you are no more than a slave.

Take the Christian religion for an example. Through Christianity you're taught to turn the other cheek, what happens? Your enemy hits you on the other one, then realizing you won't fight, he simply takes your possessions. Then, you are taught to "love" your enemy. Imagine yourself being abducted from your home; constantly beaten and tortured; watching your women get raped; your children being taken and sold, all the while "loving" the ones doing this to you. Honestly, you don't love these people, because you know they do NOT love you. You can't love them; you want to kill them. However, trying to be a "good Christian" programs you to fool yourself, to override your own feelings.

For black people, Christianity teaches that Jesus was the son of God, yet he was beaten, tortured, and ultimately killed by the government. So, you know for a fact that if God did not come to save his own son, you have no hope when the police come for you no matter how innocent you are."

Mike had smoked nearly a whole pack of cigarettes during our conversation. He never let one go out without lighting another. He fumbled with the pack, took a deep puff, then asked "well in reality white people really are blue eyed devils."

"It's an insult to some to be called a devil, but as far as the other races of man on earth are concerned, they are. You see, most whites in this country are taught from birth that they are better than others, and that God created them to dominate the other races. This causes a symbological problem called "illusions of grandeur." No other race will ever be able to get along with whites who believe this, because they carry conflict everywhere they go. How else could it be? If you honestly believe that you're supposed to control the lives of others, and the ones you want to control honestly believe that God wants them to be free, the association of the two can only bring about conflict."

"But where do white people get these ideas?"

"When I went to school in Alabama, the schools were segregated. I learned white children were taught that God created all the races of man, before he created white man. We were supposed to be too dumb to develop the earth, so God created the white man to tell us what to do. This theory, teaching was even repeated on one of the television talk shows."

"Why doesn't somebody tell the truth?"

"It's not that they don't know the truth. It's just that the only way to straighten things out is to give back everything that was stolen from the other races, the Indians and blacks. You know for yourself; they would rather die and go to hell before they do that.

Now everyone is saying, we're not responsible for what our forefathers did, while they continue to live on the stolen wealth of those same forefathers and still work to carry it out the original plan of the forefathers, the eventual elimination of the other races."

"It seems weird to me, that people with good sense would think like that, but I know one thing for sure: they are killing us off and locking us up real fast."

"Yeah, you have people that do not believe in God, but everyone believes in their idea of heaven. The white idea of heaven is a carefully controlled society. They want cameras on every street, and every house, and total control of everything that you might do or think. Then they choose the ways you call these terrorist cops or police officers but calling them different names does not make their job any different. This is why there are beatings like the Rodney King incident; shootings of innocent unarmed people, and constant harassment." The other races can work to support them while they live as gods. Their Heaven is Our Hell.

Slavery never came to an end in the United States. It just evolved when blacks were given what they call "freedom". "Without land there was no choice but to keep working for whites. What else can they do? Freed slaves have no way of getting back to the culture of their kidnapped parents. Now you have black men who go to these 'jobs' day after day, year after year, until they are dead or too old to work. They come home to watch TV, go out get drunk, and try not to think that something is wrong here.

It took me a long time and a lot of studying to find out who and what I am. I agree with those who yell: 'You don't belong here. Go back to where you came from.' I certainly would if it were that simple. I'm a lost warrior. I was captured and brought to this country so long ago, I no longer remember what my home was like, but I refused to forget that I once had a home."

"Is that why people keep talking about a race war?"

"Some have predicted a race war because of the nature of man. Some Chinese are happy to be Americans, others will never forgive or forget what was done to their people while building American railroads. Some Japanese are happy to be Americans, others will never forget the bombing of their people. Some black people are happy to be called African American and feel fortunate that they are in this country then, yeah those like me.

When one author went back to Africa to discover his roots, he was told that 'one day a hunter went out to hunt and was never seen again.' I can relate to that story. There is no way that I can forget what happened to my people during slavery, after slavery, and today.

My belief is that, if the white man knows that if any of these people were able to face them on equal terms, they will not hesitate to take revenge. Whites protect themselves by paying terrorists to spread fear through the neighborhoods of the minorities that they find threatening. You call these terrorist cops or police officers but, calling them different names does not make their job any different. This is why there are beatings like the Rodney King incident, shootings of innocent unarmed people, and constant harassment."

I pointed to the police car driving slowly by, looking in all directions to make sure that we knew we were being watched. Then I continued. "The terrorists can come into minority neighborhoods anytime they want but we can't go to theirs.

They will say that the policeman's job is to protect and serve, but they are there to protect and serve whites. The job changes when it comes to blacks and Latinos. Every child who grows up in a poor neighborhood knows that the policemen are not in their neighborhood to protect and serve them. Sometimes the truth comes out in movies like the scene in 'Forty-eight Hours' in which Nick Nolte, playing the role of a policeman, tails Eddie Murphy,' just doing my job keeping you down,' but, is just plain common sense. The abuser must keep his eyes on his victims forever. Indians will always have to be watched, blacks, Latinos, everyone who has felt abuse.

Look at the situation in Iraq. Now that Iraq has been attacked by the United States, this country will have to do everything in its power to make sure that Iraq does not develop weapons that will allow them to be on equal terms period. Now they will always have to keep Iraq down, just like us."

"Looks like we're going to have to start fighting then."

"I used to think that was the only answer. That was before I found out that there really is a God. Now I know that only answer is getting back to God. Our God. It takes time and a lot of studying, but if you look for God, you'll find that the knowledge you seek will always be made available.

Our captors fear our gods too. You'll be surprised to know the lengths they go to keep you away from your gods. If you go to church and listen to the black preacher, white supremacy it's safe.

During slavery the only black men they allowed to become preachers were those whom the whites could trust to deliver only the sermons white slave owners wanted to be preached. The programming that was done to the preachers' during slavery was inherited by our modern-day preachers.

I know now that our God never intended us to kill another creature (for any reason other than self-defense), eat dead flesh, drink blood, harm the earth, or tell any untruths. Now we find ourselves in a culture where deception is a way of life. Politicians are known for lying. Judges, lawyers, and law enforcement officers lie to incarcerate as many young blacks and Latinos as they can. News reporters lie to hide the evil deeds of the white supremacist.

In too many instances you must lie on applications to get a job. When you want to get a day off from work you must lie. You get used to lying knowing that God hates liars. Doing these things, ensures your place in hell and as far away from God as you can get."

Mary ran up to me again and told me that she was ready to go. Mike and I shook hands. He told me that he appreciated the knowledge I had shared with him. He picked up his 40 oz, started to take a drink, then changed his mind and threw the bottle into the nearby trash container.

"I feel like I've been to school, man... You should be a teacher." Mike said.

"Each one teaches one." I replied. I took Mary's hand and we walked away.

CHAPTER 2

Hell

It has always been a mystery to me how two people can look at the same thing and each one can see something completely different. I'm amazed by the fact that a single conversation with someone having a different view from yours can sometimes change one's perception.

Many people who live in or around Los Angeles know that downtown LA can be a dangerous place, especially at night. People visiting, especially from other countries, may be a little less cautious than the residents.

I found myself in downtown LA around midnight walking towards the bus stop near Spring and 6th Steet. I had just turned the corner on Spring Street when I spotted a man being forced into a doorway of a building by two other men, I ran to the scene one of the men had a knife. He quickly turned the knife towards me as I approached. I stopped and put my hands up.

"Take it easy man." I spoke. "I just ran up here to tell you guys that the police are right around the corner coming this way."

The man looked at each other nervously. "Let's get out of here," one of the robbers said. "He might be lying," the other one replied. The man with the knife turned the blade towards me, walked a few steps from the doorway and peeked around the corner. As soon

MILLION MAN MARCH

as his eyes left me, I threw a punch knocking him to the ground. His accomplice came towards me, I kicked him in the chest, he fell to the ground. The man with the knife scrambled to his feet and threw the knife at me it missed, and they both ran off.

The man who had been robbed was a little shaken, but he was not hurt. I found out that the man was tourist from France. We talked as we walked to the bus. We had about a 40-minute trip on the bus. I tried to learn as much as I could about France. He wanted to talk about LA.

"You have to be careful here," I said. "Los Angeles is a very dangerous place. You could be robbed or killed at any time here."

Although there had been an attempt to rob him, this man's doubts about Los Angeles were completely different from the ones I had formed during my stay in California.

"There are robbers all over the world, but for some people in other countries, to be able to visit Los Angeles is like a dream come true," he said.

"What makes people want to come here?" I asked.

"Here there is scientific knowledge and technology unmatched anywhere in the world. It is indeed a great honor to be able to see some of it."

I told the man that I felt strange realizing that looking at the same city all he could see was beauty. On the other hand, all I could see was ugliness. I told him about some of my negative experiences with blacks and whites. Although I had encountered some exceptions, I found Hispanics and Asians to be more Spiritual.

My first day in California, I was looking at some sites when a white man in Beverly Hills yelled out of the car and called me a nigger (common in Alabama.) I had been denied jobs because of racism; I had come face to face with blatant racists on the police force and in government offices. My apartment had been broken into more than once, as well as my car (by black people

I suspected). I had walked into apartment buildings and been immediately told that there were no vacancies because of my race. I had moved into neighborhoods where whites threw things on my porch. (I had experienced a neighborhood in Alabama where whites would turn their backs whenever I walked outside my door.) I witnessed and, have had conversations with men who had suffered beatings like the one seen in the Rodney King video. The list goes on and on.

After I finished my story, we began to discuss religious beliefs and good and evil. The man wrote down the name of a book and told me that I should read it if it was available in this country (I was always anxious to learn new things. I was excited that the book might not be available in the US).

After I met and talked to this man, I was more determined than ever to go back to school. I wanted to see for myself and to be part of the technological advances the Frenchman had spoken about. I appreciated the inspiration I received from that conversation. It was because of the conversation that I found myself taking another bus ride to California State University in Los Angeles.

I was caring for my niece at the time and the only way I could attend classes was to take her to these classes with me it would turn out to be too much for me in the end, I was not a young man.

A very disheveled man sat next to Little Mary and me on the bus. The man spoke to Mary. He seemed surprised that Mary smiled and spoke back. He told her that she was pretty. Then he asked me if he could give her a piece of gum. I told him that it was OK.

The man wore a shabby suit. Judging from his appearance, he was very poor, probably homeless. I could tell that being around people caused him to be nervous because of his condition. He felt embarrassed. I understood, having been in the same situation. Broke, hungry, dirty, dressed in clothes giving away by mission, and feeling that all eyes are on you.

"That's a beautiful little girl you have there," he said. "She has a beautiful personality too."

"She's my great niece. She's been with me most of her life though. She is more like my daughter. Isn't that right Mary?" Mary smiled and gave me a hug.

"I'm not used to people being nice." the man said. You probably can tell from the way I look that I'm homeless. Most of the time people don't speak to me. They tried to stay away and keep their children away. I haven't had a job for a long time, but you can bet your life is not because I haven't been trying. I check out everything. If I had a dollar for every application I filled out, I'd be rich."

"I've been in your shoes man," I said. "I know what you're talking about." I realized that I had found myself in a situation where this man needed someone to talk to and I was that person.

"I just left the place where they were supposed to be hiring it took me all day to get there on the bus. I go inside, there's a little racist white woman that's sitting behind a desk. She frowns when I walk in She's afraid to hand me a pencil or paper. She is afraid to take the application when I hand it back to her. Then she says, "we'll call you." As I leave, I can hear my application being crumpled and thrown away."

"I know exactly what you mean man I've been there more than one time."

"It has happened to me so many times that I feel like I'm in the twilight zone, going through the same thing over and over. I'm tired, I don't want to have to deal with white people, but I want to get myself out of the mess I'm in and I follow up on every job lead. It always ends up the same way. You must go meet some white person who acts like they are afraid you have come to rob them."

"You should not feel bad about the way other people act man. I studied a little anthropology in college. You would have to be a fool to think that black people have equal rights in this country but, just think about what the Indians and the slaves must have gone through. I guess we can be glad that things are not worse. Understand that there are blacks who succeed. Pray and keep trying. We are not the first to have this conversation."

"Why do they want to make things so hard for other people?"

"It's easy to claim that you are superior, it's just hard to prove it. If they can't keep others poor, being rich losing loses it's meaning. Without degrading other races of people, white supremacy means nothing. They will always find faults with what others do, while they're busy doing worse things themselves."

"Yeah, but we don't mean them no harm. We don't want to take anything from them, we just want to be able to survive. They act like they're afraid we want something from them."

The bus was nearing my destination. I shook hands with the man as I started for the door.

"Keep your head up man. Do what you must do to survive and don't feel guilty. Along with colonization came misery. Nothing has changed yet, but it will."

Having been raised in Alabama I was of a mindset that the southern part of the United States was the evilest place in the world. I had not been prepared for what I encountered in California but, I guess it's hard to escape evil.

I felt that God had blessed California with astounding natural beauty. Lucifer had cursed the atmosphere with an unnatural evil. It just seemed to me that acts of evil seem to me more blatant in California than in the rest of the United States, or the rest of the world.

Many Californians appeared to be shocked when the Rodney King video was shown on television. I'll bet most of them had seen something similar before. I witnessed a man being beaten by police less than a week after I moved to Los Angeles. During my stay in Los Angeles, I had travelled through a neighborhood where some young white men wore patches on their shirts that depicted little black man hanging from a tree.

In addition to that, I had met and gotten to know some black gang members who were a lot more vicious than anyone I had ever met including Marines. I met black men and Latinos who had been abused by law enforcement and laughed at when they reported it. It was sort of like the only people to report crime to are the criminals.

Growing up in Alabama we were aware that we could not trust law enforcement. Many of the ones who wore policeman uniforms were also Klan members. Some of the few black people who got a chance to work for the state government told stories about how Klan members would force them to build a cross that they would burn during their ceremonies.

During the civil rights movement black people were told; "In the future you will not have to worry about Klansmen in white robes, they will be wearing black robes." This was their way of making us aware that the judges we faced would be Klansmen. We grew up knowing that we were involved in a war whether we wanted to be or not.

As far as blacks were concerned, trying to be a good citizen didn't mean a lot. Blacks had always been the enemy. Without some extensive studying blacks were unaware of the fact that the state of California tried to bring back slavery after it had been abolished and that there were still people trying to reestablish slavery.

It was hard to ignore the fact that bills introduced by the governor of California and negative consequences for blacks and Latinos proposition 187 was aimed at Latinos. Abolishing affirmative action would resegregate the schools, and the theory that whites were created to dominate the other races, could be taught to all white classes.

To have complete domination of the earth and races, required keeping the races divided. It was both shocking and enlightening to talk to a white racist who would try to engage me into a negative conversation about Latinos.

I was taking the bus to the Veteran's Administration Brentwood hospital. When I arrived at the bus stop, I began admiring the beauty of this Latino woman seated on the bench. The lady must have somehow felt me staring at her hair (it was black, wavy, and came well below her knees.) She turned and looked straight into my eyes. I nodded a greeting to her with this shy and somewhat embarrassed smile on my face. The lady nodded and returned the smile and I felt at ease.

A car pulled up to the bus stop and dropped off a passenger, then sped off. The man who got out of the car was in uniform. At first, I thought it was a sheriff's uniform, but as he walked closer i could tell he was a security guard.

The man seemed nervous. He rushed up to me and said, "Do you know what time this bus comes?"

"No." The man paced back and forth from the bus stop to the street several times he glanced at a Taekwondo emblem that I wore on my sweatsuit.

"Taekwondo… do you practice that?"

"Yes." I answered.

"How long?"

"I guess... 20 years or so."

"I've been practicing for 25 years." He said, probably trying to convince me that he was superior.

"What is your rank?"

"I got to the black belt but, I haven't tested since the 70s."

"I'm an eighth-degree black belt," he replied. He looked at a fast-food restaurant next near the bus stop.

"Do you think I have time to get a burger before the bus comes?"

"I really don't have any idea how this bus runs."

"Well, I'm going to run in here and see. If you see the bus coming, would you signal me through the window?"

"Sure." He ran into the restaurant.

It seemed like it was less than a minute before the security guard ran back out of the restaurant.

"Look... I just want to know one thing... I am not prejudice or nothing, but why are Mexicans so damned slow?"

The lady on the bench winced when she heard the statement. I felt embarrassed, uncomfortable and somewhat angered. I frowned as I answered.

"How fast would you work for minimum wages?"

The man lowered his voice and dropped his head.

"Minimum wages. Yes. I see what you mean."

The lady on the bench turned and gave me a big smile. The more I thought about what I had been asked, the more upset I became.

The guard did not say much of anything else until the bus came. Then he told me that he did not have enough change for the bus and asked if he could borrow a quarter.

When we boarded the bus, I took a seat near the front. The guard walked towards the back. He thanked me for the quarter I was thinking of questions I wanted to ask the man.

Although blacks and Latinos were thought to be less intelligent than whites, what would make him think that I was too dumb to realize what he was trying to do? The more I thought about it, the angrier I became. The old "divide and conquer" trick, I thought. When racist is around Latinos, they degrade blacks and Asians, when they're around blacks they degrade Latinos and Asians. When they are around Asians, they degrade blacks and Latinos.

I remember whites using the same trick in the 50s and 60s, but it goes back further than that. What would make him think that people would not be aware of it by now?

New generations come along, each hoping and believing that there is some honesty in government while the white supremacy remain in power manipulating minds with movies, TV, radio, and newspapers.

Just as politician gained the help of blacks with proposition 187 by convincing them that Latinos were coming here illegally and taking their jobs, they try to get help from Asians in abolishing affirmative action by convincing them that more of them would have the opportunity to attend school were it not for Affirmative Action. One thing that I had learned in my travels was, most people get along well when they feel that they have equal opportunities, and no one cares about who is superior.

I felt that Affirmative Action was brought about because of unfair treatment of minorities by whites. Whites quickly found a way to get around it. The unfair treatment continued, there was no real enforcement of Affirmative action, and many believed that the ones who benefited most were white women.

During this time, the governor of California was saying that he did not believe in preferential treatment for anyone, and that Affirmative Action is preferential treatment. There were stories about those who have been receiving preferential treatment since the 1980s to get into schools like UCLA, from the same people who were trying to do away with Affirmative Action, like the governor himself.

There was something called the "Three Strikes Law" that had been put into effect in California. This law had not been in effect for long but there were already reports of whites finding ways around the law while blacks and Latinos were marched off to prison with little hope of ever seeing freedom again.

One example of the way the law was enforced was reported in the news. A white man, faced with "Three Strikes Law," aborted life in prison out to stealing a car while a black man was sentenced to life in prison under the same law for stealing a slice of pizza.

The one sure thing about the politicians is, you never know what they plan to do by what they say. However, their actions speak loudly. The "Three Strikes – You're Out" Law reintroduced Slavery without calling it Slavery.

There seemed to be a well thought out plan going into effect: kill Affirmative Action and no one will be obligated to hire minorities. The rate of unemployment for blacks is already high and this is a sure way to increase it. Welfare has been cut to the point where no one can survive/live off it. Most of the men will be forced into crime just to supply their basic human needs. In the meantime, the government brags about Spending $36 million on a space project.

Big companies now invest in prisons. Prisoners (who have been sentenced to life by the "Three Strikes Law") have no hope of freedom. Legislation is introduced to eliminate all rights of prisoners and the plan is complete, a reemergence of the institution created by Lucifer himself and perpetuated by his followers, **Slavery**. It is a demonic practice to seek profit from the misery of others, yet the facts are there.

The mayor of Los Angeles was reported to be investigating the decreasing number of arrests in Los Angeles. Black people felt that a decrease in the number showed that the new police chief was doing a good job. The mayor looked at the situation as being negative. If you make deals with companies to invest in prisons, you try to find ways to get prisoners. The word on the streets was that the mayor was under pressure to produce "slaves" to make their investments in the prisons pay off.

In the days of slavery, black slaves would run away to the northern states to find freedom from oppression. As I jogged along the beach looking out over the ocean, I realized that this was the end. I left Montgomery, Alabama hoping that I could escape racism by moving to Detroit, Michigan. Realizing that racism is just as alive in the North as it is in the South. I moved West to California only to find racism is more prevalent than it is in the North or the South. There is no longer a "North" to run to.

Eventually you reach the realization that there is nowhere to go. The earth that God created no longer exists. For all indigenous people, the earth has been transformed to Hell by colonization.

While I was growing up in the South, black neighborhoods were under attack by policemen, the KKK or, just average southern white American citizens. Churches were being bombed, innocent women and children were being killed while praying. Black men were being lynched for things like whistling at white women, men were being shot or beaten to death by the police for wandering into white neighborhoods. The only thing we were sure of was the statement, "life is short."

None of the young men I grew up with were expected to live past the age of 17, but it didn't really matter the quicker you die the better. Death seemed to be the only way out. There would probably have been an epidemic of suicides were it not for the fact that we were raised to be Christians. We were told that suicide was an unforgivable sin and one sure way of going to hell.

The earth was bad enough for me. I did not want to even think of going to a worse place. Eventually I volunteered for the Marine Corps as what was called a Vietnam replacement. I felt that if I got killed there it would be a death with honor.

Some advised staying away from crime, getting a good education, and becoming employed was the answer. That was and is far from the truth in the United States. On jobs is where many minorities find themselves face to face with the racists and the realization that whites will never consider equality for non-whites. By a country that grew from white supremacy, there is no equality.

In Alabama, I watched my mother work until she was sick, in the homes of whites for $0.50 an hour. My stepfather and his black coworkers did highly skilled construction work for salaries of $1.00 an hour or less. They worked hard for long hours day after day while whites came to the job and were paid high salaries for nothing more than standing around talking about their new cars, homes, and great salaries.

Even in hell some people resist the devil. Many young blacks can see what is waiting for them by observing their parents. They refused to go through the process of studying hard to learn a profession only to find out that because of the way the system is set up, they can only advance as far as the whites are willing to let them go. Which is not far at all, because they feel they must stay ahead.

The black men who refused to submit to white supremacy eventually end up imprisoned or dead. The only important thing to whites is that blacks work for them. That was the purpose of bringing blacks to this country. They were to be the burden bearers for whites. Those who will not do it willingly are killed or forced to work in prisons at gunpoint.

There are blacks who sell their souls. They go to schools, putting up with the racism in the schools, then get employed, putting up with racism on the jobs, eventually telling themselves that they are doing the right thing. Some even want to be considered role models for our children because they go to work every day.

After a person closes his mind for a long period of time, the receptors become damaged, and he finds himself incapable of dealing with the truth. Athletes are looked up to and respected by the young. However, like slaves, these men are owned, and their actions are carefully controlled by these owners who sometimes refer to them as "trained monkeys."

Others have become successful in business or entertainment, but everything they work for can be destroyed. James Cleveland "Jesse" Owens won four gold medals at the 1936 Olympic games.

However, his treatment in the United States turned out to be more of a horror story than anything else.

During the Jim Crow era, John Arthur Johnson or "Jack Johnson" became the first black world heavyweight boxing champion. In the United States his success was seen as threatening to the myth of white supremacy and he was said to have been forced into exile.

I find it amazing that it's hard to get away from racist incidents or racist conversations. It seems as if it's been like that all my life. The same day that the white man asked me "why are Mexicans so damn slow" I arrived at the VA hospital in Brentwood to encounter an even more interesting situation.

I was in the waiting room with one other black man and a white man. The three of us began talking about women. The white man was excited that he was having an affair with a woman who he claimed was young enough to be his daughter. In fact, he said there she was a friend of his daughters. He was anxious to get the doctor's visit over so that he could meet the girl.

While we were laughing and talking, a young well-dressed black man walked into the room. We could not ignore the fact that he was very angry. He looked at the white man, walked towards him and asked, "why are you here?"

"I beg your pardon."

"I said why are you here? Don't try to pretend that you don't know what I'm talking about. You white people have cheated everyone and stolen everything from everybody. This hospital is supposed to be for veterans who need help. Now why the fuck are you here?"

I smiled but I said nothing. The other black man who was there got nervous also. He tried to calm the other man down.

"Chill out brother. It's going to be all right."

"Chill out my ass. I am just tired of white people, man. I can't take it anymore." The man took a seat next to me and continued to speak.

"Look man, I studied hard in college and worked hard to get this job. I worked hard on the job. Last week I was up for promotion. I had seniority, education, and I was the all-around best qualified person for the job, no question. So, what happened? They bring in some white boy, a relative of one of the managers, and gave him the job that I was supposed to be promoted to. The thing is, the guy has none of the qualifications for the job, none whatsoever. He never even finished high school. I lost it, I went off. I wanted to kill a bunch of white people, man. So, they sent me out here. I'm supposed to see a psychiatrist. They fuck you over, and when you go off, you are the one who's crazy."

"Look, man, the white man said, "I have no idea what you're talking about. I am no better off than you."

"Fuck you! All of you are the same, damned blue-eyed devils."

"Hold on, man, the other black man said. "Try to take it easy."

"Take it easy! Take it easy! Do you know how hard I worked in school? Do you know how hard I worked on that job only to see some white motherfucker getting handed something for nothing? On top of that, this white boy is supposed to supervise me! Fuck that!"

The man looked over at me. "Yeah, man, I see your martial arts patch. I took a little of that too. It's supposed to help you find inner peace. How in the hell do you find inner peace when the whites are blatantly messing over us every day?"

"I know how things are, but no one in this room is your enemy."

The other black man spoke. "We are trying to find our way out of this mess just like you. I have run into problems trying to make it on those jobs as well and I don't want to be a criminal that is why it's very important to me to get my 100% disability so that I can take care of my family."

The angry man looked towards me again. "Is that the answer? Just let them label you as being crazy, take the little disability, and keep your mouth shut. In the meantime, they are fucking over entire races of people and trying to fool everyone like there is some kind of equal opportunity here. Is being crazy the answer?"

I shook my head, smiled, and placed my hand on the man's shoulder. "Hang in there, man, you got to hang in there."

I wanted to tell him that in the 1960s, I was in the exact position he was in now. It was a shock but not a surprise to find the same things going on jobs in the 90s.

I wanted to tell him that I had never really found an answer, but I did learn as much as I could about how we got into this situation and that was the beginning of understanding...

I want to tell him that I had become so angry at one point that I was ready to take on the whole white race myself, but common sense tells you the odds are too great and some others who have tried did not turn out well. Other blacks who have accepted their situations, will not protest for fear of losing those jobs and, the men willing to fight, end up imprisoned, dead, drug addicts or mental patients like us.

I wanted to tell this young man a lot of things, but I did not say too much. It was not long before some men came into the room to take the man away. I wondered if he would live long enough to learn the things I had learned, and for the first time in my life I felt guilty about not saying more.

The man looked around at me as he was being led away. "You know what I think?" I think that we are all dead men, and this is hell."

CHAPTER 3

The last great African American hero

There are laws regulating discrimination and racism in the workplace, but to whom does the victimized person report violations? In most cases, the so-called "minorities" how to report racist actions against them by whites, to other whites. Most of the time, no action is taken, and the situation is covered up.

I remember watching a talk show on TV when a white man was telling about being hired as an apartment manager. The owner of the building had a certain section reserved for blacks to rent.

While the black tenants were away from their apartments, the building owner would enlist the aid of the manager to damage the apartments. They would then go to court and sue the black tenant for the damages they had done.

The manager reported these actions to the mayor of the city. The man said that he was told by the mayor that if he was a white man reporting another white man for discrimination, he was the one with the problem.

The abuse of non-whites through racist action goes on day after day, year after year. Young people find themselves faced with the same situations that their parents experienced and their parents before them, all the way back to the time when blacks were brought here as slaves.

I was not surprised at the racism I encountered in the Marine Corps I was surprised to watch a TV news report showing the same racism in the 90s that I had experienced in the 60s. The white officers still use the same racist statements as there aren't a lot of black officers because they have found that blacks do not swim or shoot as well as whites.

The most disturbing thing is that you can always find a black person to speak on behalf of whites. That is why the so-called "token" is so important to white supremacy. It is comical but sad to see a black marine officer say that he believes that there is equal opportunity in the military when some white officers would tell the truth about the racial situation.

I was discharged from the Marine Corps in 1967. I returned home with physical and mental problems. These problems were not caused by war. Minorities in the military often found themselves in an unexpected war, a war against racism.

While serving as a machine gunner and having problems with my feet and ankles. I eventually had to go to doctors who told me that I had lost the arch in my feet and would probably be discharged. I was placed on light duty.

I ended up under the command of an officer who said that he did not believe in light duty (for minorities). It was a strange situation, I found myself being punished for being placed on light duty. Instead of light duty, this officer increased my assignments and actually made sure that I was assigned to do more than the other marines.

On several occasions I was called to the office of the commanding officer. He did not show up for hours, but some white marines were there taunting me while I waited.

"The reason you have problems with your feet is because they don't wear shoes down in Alabama." Some would say. I would sometimes find myself ordered to stand at attention for hours while white marines told "nigger jokes".

I was an M60 machine gunner. The weapon weighed 60 lbs. or more. I was a fire team leader and members of a team would take turns carrying the weapon on long trips. The commanding officer made a decision that I was not to get any help carrying the weapon. While other marines were relieved about every two miles on ten-mile hikes to the range, I was ordered to carry the weapon alone the entire ten miles.

I learned to live in constant pain, day and night. To this day my left shoulder still hurts from the weight of the M60 machine gun. Even when we did not go to the range, I was ordered to carry the weapon everywhere I went. The other marines could not understand the punishment, but I became well respected for successfully completing my missions.

The proudest days of my life were during my service in the Marine Corps. I can never forget graduating from boot camp. An officer gave a speech at the graduation ceremony saying, "These men have earned the right to be called Marine, and once a Marine, always a Marine." From that moment on the word "nigger" lost its sting.

The second time I felt extremely proud was when I was approached by a Black Officer who could not understand why I had been ordered to carry that machine gun everywhere when no one else had to.

"Don't worry," he told me. "If you can do it I guarantee you'll be twice as tough as any marine that ever came through the corps."

I was able to function in extreme pain and from that time no other man from any race could make me feel bad about myself. As a result of this situation the joints in my ankle began to fuse together and when I was discharged the doctors were careful to conceal this condition in order to prevent me from receiving compensation.

The condition of my feet continued to grow worse after I was discharged, and I had to eventually get help from President Jimmy Carter to have my case reopened from the time I was discharged. The effort that the Department of Veterans Affairs made to prevent paying the disability compensation provided by law, should be a hate crime.

If there was ever an investigation into the ways minority veterans were robbed of the benefits provided by laws, it would cause minorities to think twice about entering military service for the United States. I was unable to walk or work because of disabilities from the United States Marine Corps when the sheriffs came to put me out of my home. I felt alone, however, it wasn't long before I encountered other homeless veterans. Some had horror stories greater than mine.

I found that I could survive on the streets because I had been taught survival by the Marine Corps. For me, being homeless was one of the worst things that could ever happen. I was very poor during my youth, but never homeless. My main desire was to get a roof over my head and a normal job. I was far too embarrassed about my situation to let my family know what I was going through. The most embarrassing part was that: my situation was caused by my service in the United States Marine Corps.

It would be hard to explain how amazed I was when I encountered a group of veterans who had become so disgusted with the Department of Veterans affairs that they no longer wanted any parts of the United States government. The most amazing part for me was that some of them were white.

After being discharged from the Marine Corps I moved back to Montgomery AL. That was like going from the frying pan to the fire. Extreme racism in Alabama from whites along with black gang violence was the reason I had enlisted in the marines in the first place. An example of what life was like in the South was put into music in a song by Nina Simone called "Mississippi Goddam". To this day I feel like no human being should ever encounter the situations we had to face. There was no comfort in being told that slaves and indigenous Americans were victims of worse evil treatment.

Black gangs and a lot of dangerous black people; poverty and desperation had made them that way. But nothing could compare to the violence of whites. That was a good possibility that you could be robbed and killed by blacks. In addition to that you might be lynched by whites for their entertainment. For me volunteering to go to war seemed the safest choice.

When I left, there was the feeling that blacks were beginning to unite in marches and a lot of them were coming together in protest. I remember Doctor Martin Luther King marching through poverty-stricken neighborhoods gathering crowds as he marched. The song "We Shall Overcome" was popular with the marchers. Encounters with law enforcement were brutal.

Blacks were desperate to get equal rights, whites were desperate to make sure that we did not. Attack dogs, water hoses, and brutal police beatings were too much of an advantage over those whose only weapon were songs. I, along with some of my peers, did not understand why we were being told not to fight back. It would have been a losing battle though, there was an overwhelming weapons advantage. It's just that I could not see the honor in letting oneself be beaten without fighting back or in being evil enough to prefer killing people rather than giving them freedom.

When I returned some of the "whites only" signs had been removed in government buildings although some remained in private businesses. Some buildings found themselves with extra restrooms and water fountains because they were built with two of everything. One for whites, one for blacks.

Black veterans like me, who had served in the military during the Vietnam era, were able to get government jobs. I began working for the Veterans' Administrations Regional Office in Alabama. There were some whites who were terribly upset, others were quite friendly.

Blacks had to support each other and warn each other to keep calm when confronted with those who hated blacks and tried to intimidate us on the job. Those government jobs meant a lot to black workers. And in places where there was so much poverty, some blacks were now able to buy homes and cars. Eventually the jobs became so important that the racist practices were ignored.

Whites in supervisory positions could create jobs for their friends and relatives. They did. Jobs could be upgraded and raises given whenever they wanted to. Blacks were always kept at a certain level and very few were hired at that time.

I became almost uncontrollably angry on several occasions. I probably would have lost my job had it not been for the older black man who worked there. They would always talk to me and calm me down. I had a lot of respect for the older black men.

I had been hired on some type of program in which I had to obtain at least one year of college to maintain my position. I was not eligible for any promotion for one year.

After I had worked there for about nine months, a white man was hired at a grade below me. Within two months he was promoted to two grades above me. By this time, I was well into completing my year of college. The man who had been hired and not completed high school.

I remember the young white man coming to work bragging about his new Trans Am. I was unable to afford a bicycle and was told that because he came in on a different program he could be promoted, I could not.

I was in the same position as the man I had met and spoke about at the veteran's administration hospital in California. I found myself wanting to kill everything white. I was already familiar with how racist Alabama was and that I could not get any help on a local or state level. As a Vietnam era veteran, I wrote about the situation to the president at that time.

It was the 60s, a time of black awareness and black pride. I knew that I could count on my brothers to back me up. Then I began to see the reality of racism.

The wife of the well-known racist, George Wallace (Mrs. Lurleen Wallace) had died and supervisors we're collecting donations from the employees for a fund for Mrs. Wallace. The black men then got together immediately and held a conference.

"Do they actually expect us to donate money to Lurleen Wallace? Isn't she the one who ordered the national guardsmen to shoot to kill when blacks were demonstrating?"

"I am not that stupid. If someone comes to me for a donation, I'm going to tell them to go to hell."

We laughed and joked about the donation for Mrs. Wallace. Each of us swore that we would not give any money. I happened to be the first one my supervisor approached about the donation. I was still fired up from our black conference.

"We're collecting money for a fund for Mrs. Lurleen Wallace," the supervisor said. "Would you like to donate?"

"Lurline Wallace!" I shouted. "Hell no!"

The supervisor smiled and walked away. He approached the other black man. To my surprise, every other black man there gave a donation, after they had sworn that they would not.

I was not angry. I understood why the men felt that they had to donate money though they did not want to. They felt that they were living good compared to other blacks, they had families to support, mortgage payments, car payments, and the last thing they wanted to do was to make waves on the job.

I saw how people would actually sell their souls to escape the situations we had lived in however, I lost respect for those men. For me they had been the last great black American heroes. Men who became educated and employed by the government. Men who were to be held up as examples to the young black men who grew up with nothing more than the feeling of hopelessness. In reality, to keep their positions and to maintain what they had gained they had to bow to white supremacy.

I left Alabama and moved to Detroit to join the Police Department. It was seven years before I received a reply to my application. During that time I went to work for the Veterans Administrations Regional Office in Detroit.

It was not long before I found out that racism on the job in Detroit was different from that in Alabama because it was more hidden. On one occasion the black employees were shocked when a new employee was called to the personnel office for a conference. The man was black, but he looked white. The personnel officer thought that the man was white, they called him to the office to give him some pointers on how to act towards and around blacks. His story got around to all of the black employees.

I went to work for Chrysler corporation. I also met Grandmaster Shim and began learning the art of Taekwondo. I became completely engrossed in my Taekwondo training for nearly seven years. I was oblivious to social problems during that time. The physical training helped me to deal with the pain in my feet and legs. The mental training helped me to become a disciplined man. More important than anything else, Grandmaster Shim was the first man I had ever met that I could respect as what I thought a man should be.

MILLION MAN MARCH

I had trained in taekwondo and worked for Chrysler corporation for nearly seven years when police officers came to my apartment asking if I was still interested in police work. I told him that I was. They informed me that there had been discrimination in the hiring of police officers in Detroit and that they were going back to talk to applicants who had been denied jobs because of their race.

Maybe seven years was too long for me to stay out of trouble. When I had a background check, I was told that I could not begin working because I was behind on child support payments.

I was confused and did not know about the child that I was supposed to have fathered. I had made sure that my support payments were up to date for my two children. It was impossible for me to explain that the woman who said I was the child's father was my ex-wife, someone I had not seen for over five years. We were divorced and she had been re-married for at least three years with a two-year-old, her new husband being the father. There was no way the child could be mine.

The Police Department told me to straighten the matter out. I talked to the mother of the child and told her that my job depended on having her tell the truth to the friend of the court. She agreed however, I did not know that she worked for the police department, neither did I know that she held a grudge against me and was using the court to get even.

I went to the Police Department to tell them that they had made a mistake and that my ex-wife was willing to tell the court that she was re-married, and that the child was not mine. An old wrinkle white man with white hair leaned close to my face and said "listen nigger, that Lady does not tell the judge what to do the judge tells her what to do. If they say you owe child support, you owe child support. I was too stupid to understand that I was being set up. Had I known, I would have requested a DNA test immediately.

After I got involved with this case, I began to learn that child support was big business. The court was filled with men, mostly black who were facing the judges and having money deducted from their paychecks.

Some fathers did owe money for child support. On the other hand, some women had found that taking men to court for child support was a foolproof way of getting revenge whether they were the fathers or not. By being employed by the Police Department, my ex-wife held all of the cards. She knew the police officers, judges and court staff.

The judges were having fun with these cases. Some men were being told that they had to come up with money even if they had to start selling dope. Once a man was in the system it was nearly impossible to escape. Men who had obtained decent paying jobs with the automobile industry found themselves leaving the state to avoid the court system. In some cases, black men were ordered to pay unreasonably large payments. For these men employment was no longer gainful, but they lived under the threat that warrants would be issued if the payments were not made.

The court warned us that after three arrests we will be charged with a felony and end up serving time in prison. We learned that sometimes staying out of trouble and working hard was not the answer. If the right people wanted it just being the father of a child could become a crime.

For me, having to go to court made no sense. I was not the father of the child that they were accusing me of fathering. I also had all of the proof in the world. I was not worried until I actually got to court. There in court, my ex-wife obviously knew the judge and had obviously discussed the case with him.

When I asked the judge why I was there, he told me that I was there because I was behind on child support payments. I told him that I was up to date on my child support payments, and that

I had proof. "Yes," the judge replied. "You are making payments for two children but, you're not paying for Antone." I lost my temper because I had never heard of an Antone.

"Who the hell is Antone!" I looked at my ex-wife and the judge smiled at each other. I told the judge that I had no idea what he was talking about, and that a DNA test would prove that I was not the father of an Antone. That was my first time even hearing that name. Without the mention of my request for a DNA test, the judge immediately ordered me to be locked up.

I was in jail planning an escape when an old girlfriend bailed me out. I did not know how unreasonable the payments could become until I returned to work and found all of my paychecks being taken. I was in a bad situation. No lawyer would believe that I had been jailed without a DNA test. My insistence that I was not the father of that child made it appear that I was just another deadbeat dad trying to avoid paying child support. The irony was I could even understand how they felt that way. It was a setup, but I have to admit that it was a masterful setup. It took me 30 years to bring out the truth.

> *(After 30 years of lawyers refusing to look at the case and being hounded and harassed by the friend of the court with claims of ever increasing past due payments, I found a congressman who looked into the case to find that I had been illegally imprisoned, denied a DNA test and billed with payments that I did not owe.*
>
> *When the congressman ordered the case back into court. My ex-wife was there alone with an officer of the friend of the court. They both became nervous when I asked for a DNA test again and informed them that I had been locked up after being denied a DNA test in the first place, they immediately dropped the charges.*

Since we still had to go before the judge, the officer for the friend of the court informed me that I had better keep my mouth shut or I would end up in prison. The only one who got a chance to speak was the friend of the courts representative that had threatened me. The judge was confused as to why the charges were dropped but the friend of the court did not give him an explanation. Lawyers still refused to take the case when I tried to sue the courts.)

Because space was limited when I was ordered to jail, I was placed in maximum security. I got a chance to talk to men who did not mind robbing, killing, or raping. I knew that I was in the wrong place, and I began to wonder about other black men who had found themselves in my situation without committing a crime.

I could not control my anger. I wished that I had taken a weapon into the courtroom to attack the judge. I was damaged mentally. I felt that the judge and the court system were the criminals. I had begun making plans to escape. I felt that I would have been able to relax if I had been locked up for committing a crime.

Upon returning to work I found that so much had been deducted from my paychecks that I could not afford transportation to and from work. I could not pay rent or eat. The more I tried to explain my situation to lawyers the more I found out how lawyers stayed away from these cases. Once you are labeled a deadbeat dad, that's all they see, a deadbeat dad. I had no choice but to move away from Michigan. I moved to California.

The power that my ex-wife had by working for the Police Department made me see the importance of obtaining a job as a police officer. With a badge and a gun, you could meet the racist on equal terms and protect your people. It seemed that some whites had declared war on blacks even before they decided to make slaves. That war goes on. The problem is that, only certain types of black men can obtain that type of employment. For example, the one black police officer present during the Rodney King beating witnessed the word nigger being used over and over, but he had to swear to them that he had not heard it. His job depended on it.

I applied for a job with the Los Angeles Police Department. After I had passed the test, I was called in for an interview. This was called the oral test period. I was surprised that I was only asked one significant question. The question when something like, "if you see a police officer committing a crime, would you report them?"

I had heard about a code of silence. However, my feelings were that a police officer's job was to enforce the law. I felt that the answer "yes" was the correct answer. I was wrong. Someone came out to tell me that I had failed the oral test. I was both disappointed and at the same time, somewhat relieved. During my short stay in California, I had learned to fear these men.

I had been staying in a rundown motel on Adams Blvd. I told the owner that I was looking for work, and he let me manage the place. I had been there only two days when I heard noises coming from the alley behind the motel late one night.

When I walked into the alley, I witnessed a sight that made me dizzy. There were about eight cops there surrounding and severely beating this skinny black man with nightsticks. When I walked closer, one of the officers pointed his gun at my head and told me to get the fuck out of there. It took me a while to regain my composure. And never forget one female officer holding up a shotgun and placing her foot on the head of the man lying unconscious on the ground as if she was posing for a picture.

Two days after that, I went to check out loud talking from one of the upstairs rooms period two police officers had gone to a room looking for a man who had moved a few days earlier. A young couple had taken the room. The policeman insisted that the young couple knew something about the man who had moved. The man tried to explain that he and his wife had just moved here from out of town.

There was an argument. I walked closer to see if I could give some information that might help. One of the officers told the man that if he ever caught him outside of that room, he would kill him. When I reached the door one of the officers pointed a gun to my head again and said, "Get the fuck away from here, this is police business."

The police officers returned several times to harass the same couple. They moved. When I got to know others in the community, I learned more about police harassment and about beatings carried out by police officers some wearing KKK arm bands.

I got a job as a bus driver for the Southern California rapid transit district. This was a perfect opportunity to learn about the people and places in and around Los Angeles. I loved the job, but there was no getting around the culture shock.

Some of the black drivers were trying to change routes because when they drove through white neighborhoods they were threatened by young whites. Black and white drivers were sometimes threatened when they drove through neighborhoods that were in gang territory.

I had a conversation with an injured man who approached the bus stating that he had just gotten out of jail and did not have the money for a ride.

"What happened to you?"

"I was in jail man. The sheriffs here come to the cells at night, take you out, and beat you with those flashlights. They call it flashlight therapy."

"Beat you for what?"

"For nothing."

"You mean they just randomly pick somebody and take them to a room and beat them?"

"That is exactly what I'm saying."

"I don't understand that. You could sue them, can't you?"

"Let me tell you how it is here in California. The cops here do whatever they want. If you talk about suing them, you get threatened, your wife, children, and anybody else in your family. Don't make the mistake of thinking they don't carry these threats out."

Another bus driver was stopped by the police and beaten before a busload of passengers because he disagreed with the officer who accused him of speeding.

I was talking to a young couple who boarded my bus. I noticed a scar on the man's face. I asked him what had happened. The man said that he and his girlfriend were driving by a scene where the police were beating someone. The man yelled out of the car. "Leave him alone."

The man was surprised to see that some of the officers had gotten into their car to follow them they were pulled over that man was taken from the car and beaten. He said that his girlfriend talked him into going to the police station to file a report for police brutality. The man said that the policeman behind the desk refused to take his brutality report and told him, "You had better be glad that it wasn't me. You would be in worse shape."

The things you hear, no matter how horrible, cannot compare with the things you see. It was hard to think about policemen who would beat people for taunting them, but I got a chance to see it firsthand while driving the bus down Santa Monica Blvd. A man gave two police officers the finger as he boarded the bus.

Before I had driven three more blocks, the officers had gotten into their car and were signaling the bus to stop. When I pulled over, the officers boarded the bus, located the man who had given them the finger, and began to drag him from the bus as he yelled for help.

Strange things happen at night. I was parked across from a nightclub when I saw two Latinos being pulled out of the club by two white men. Outside the club a fight started between the men and the Latinos we're winning. One of the white men ran inside the club and yelled something.

Then a bunch of white men ran outside to help with the fight. The Latinos managed to knock a few of them down and eventually got away.

Shortly after that incident, a young man boarded the bus wearing a sweatsuit and carrying a gym bag. He sat on the seat behind me and began making motions with his hands as if he were shadow boxing. A white man, seated near the young man, began to speak.

"Say man, I see you up there making the motions with your hands. Are you trying to tell me something?"

"Are you talking to me?"

"Yeah."

"No, I'm not trying to tell you anything, man I'm just coming from the gym, I practice boxing."

"Well, I thought you were trying to tell me something. Looks like you were making motions this way. I don't care what you know. You mess with me, you get your ass kicked."

The young black man became irritated.

"I swear I just don't understand white people. They can never leave you alone. I go to the gym I practice boxing every day. I want to be a fighter. I never mess with anybody. I try to respect everyone. White people just have to bother you, no matter what you do."

I noticed another white man, seated near the center of the bus, opened his coat to check for his gun. He closed his jacket then spoke.

"Now we're not going to start talking about white people because all of us will get into this thing."

I stopped the bus and turned to look at the situation, besides myself and the young black man who had been harassed, there were two other blacks on the bus. Whites had us outnumbered about four to one. in addition, the white man who had started the disagreement was well over 6 feet tall and weighed over 200 lbs. The young black man hardly weighed 150 lbs. The big white man spoke after the man with the gun.

You don't have to worry man. I'll kick every nigger's ass on this bus."

I pulled over, put on the parking brake and turn to face the man.

"I don't know what's going on here. This sounds like something out of the 1960s to me. Now let me explain something to all of you. I'm in charge of the bus, so I'll be in charge of the ass kicking. If this conversation continues, I will clear everyone from this bus, understand?" No one spoke after that.

There was another occasion when I had just come to work and was driving an empty bus to the layover zone where my route would began as I turned the corner I was flagged down by a female bus driver.

"Can you help me please?"

"What's the problem?"

"I can't get this man off the bus."

I parked and walked on to the lady's bus. A man was seated in the back. He was dressed like a homeless person. I walked towards him.

"Sir you will have to leave the bus now."

"Fuck you! You and that black bitch. You both can go to hell for all I care."

"I don't care what you call me, as long as you leave this bus. I would appreciate it if you didn't disrespect the lady though."

"Make me leave nigger."

I walked towards the man, stood directly in front of him and made a fist. I have big hands. "You're going to leave right now or,

I am going to burst your face open. Now you get up, walk towards that door, don't turn around and don't miss a step. Every time you turn around, I'm going to drop you. Every time you miss a step, I'm going to drop you. Now move."

The man got up and yelled out a few more "niggers" as he walked to the door. He never turned around and he never missed a step. The lady thanked me, and I asked her if she had those problems often.

"You'd be surprised."

The surprises never stopped coming while driving in downtown Los Angeles, I was confronted by an angry man who claimed I had cut him off when I pulled away from the bus zone. I apologized, then told him that most drivers speed up to keep the buses from pulling away from the curb, as he had done. However, the buses have to come out and we make sure that it is safe before we do so. The man was still angry. He pulled over a motorcycle cop, told him, "That nigger pulled out in front of me." The policeman wrote me a ticket.

As with any other job, you have to deal with politics along with work. Eventually you find that whites (And sometimes well-trained blacks) in positions of management work hard to keep up the impression that blacks are inferior. And doing so, job records are tampered with. You find that blacks are reported for violations that whites would not be. Since some of the violations are minor. The supervisor will tell the black person not to worry about it, it means nothing.

Eventually you find yourself with enough minor violations to get fired. Racist whites are quick to say that blacks are not capable of filling these positions, when in fact the records of the whites who do the same thing as blacks are kept clean. A black person will be written up for anything, especially by black supervisors who, (like the government employees) know that holding these positions require bowing to white supremacy.

MILLION MAN MARCH

Many blacks and Latinos find themselves under attack in every part of their lives. Rich whites with expensive cars joke about Latinos and blacks who can't afford automobile insurance. Knowing that the uninsured driver fears having an accident, cars are used as means of intimidation.

You constantly see cars cutting off unexpected drivers. Everyone is too important not to be first. You see a mad race from intersections with four way stops. While trying to pull away from the curb or out of the driveway, you see cars speeding up to prevent others from coming out ahead of them.

It is a well-known fact that blacks and Latinos get pulled over by police more than whites, but I don't think the public knows that giving undeserved traffic tickets has become another part of the culture.

I was leaving a girlfriend's house in Lynnwood early one morning when I was stopped by two sheriff officers a male and a female. I had no idea why I was being stopped. I was riding a motorcycle. I had just pulled out of the garage and driven straight to the street. The male officer told me, "I'm writing you a ticket for driving on the sidewalk."

"I just came right out that garage on to the street. There's no way for me to get to the street without crossing the sidewalk."

"I don't give a damn what you say. I'm writing you a ticket for driving on the sidewalk." The female officer was laughing uncontrollably. If I had not realized it before, I knew for sure now, that whites in California feel like they are in a war, and you could be attacked at any time by the white citizens or by the policeman who protect them. These people actually feel good about abusing minorities and any way they can. Writing and illegal traffic tickets were even considered a victory.

On one occasion, I believe that I was about to be the victim of one of those police beatings, had it not been for a friend who was also a gang member. I was coming out of my apartment with a bag of clothes headed for the laundry. I was stopped by two big cops in uniform but in an unmarked car. They searched me, asked for ID, then placed me inside the car. Neither of the men answered when I asked if I was being arrested, if so what for and where we were going.

Just as the car was about to pull off, my friend drove up and asked what was going on. At first, they said that it was police business and told him that he had better move on.

"Bull shit! You can bet your white ass if he is going anywhere, we are going to." Several other cars pulled up.

The policemen became nervous. They said that they saw me coming out of the apartment with the bag of clothes and thought that I was a burglar. My friend asked where they were taking me. They told him that they could not release me on the street and that I would have to be taken to the station.

He told me that he would follow me. The policemen drove off with a caravan of gang members following. I was driven to the back of some police station, then released.

My friend picked me up and told me that he felt obligated to follow me because he had been picked up and beaten by some white cops who were wearing the KKK arm bands. He told me how frustrated he became when he tried to report the incident. No one would listen.

In comparing life and the level of racism in Alabama, Michigan, Texas and California. I found that California was by far the most racist state and some of the most blatant racist acts occurred there. Like my friend said, no one listens unless you're white.

Bus drivers, with the empty buses sometimes like to race to the layover zones. Everyone knew that it was against company policy, but it was done. I raced with a white bus driver, not realizing that I was not supposed to win. The driver did pass me once, but my bus was faster, so I easily got around him and wound up in the lead.

The driver was furious. He could not stand losing, even a stupid little bus race. He swore he would get even. The next day I was summoned to the manager's office. The white driver who had lost the race, had submitted an accident report, claiming that I had hit his bus as I passed him and had broken off a mirror. I was asked if I had had an accident. I was bewildered.

The manager, along with all the mechanics, checked my bus from top to bottom. They were unable to find even the smallest scratch. I will never forget the look of bewilderment on the manager's face. I could not have hit the other driver's bus without some type of evidence.

The manager could not understand what had happened or why the man would write the false report. He looked at me as if he thought that I knew something that I was not telling but there was no way that the other driver's story could hold up.

In another incident, a white man seated behind me started yelling for me to slow down. I ignored him at first, but his yelling increased. "I said slow this bus down, you fucking nigger."

I stopped, parked the bus, then approach the man. "Look, I can't drive the bus the way you want me to, I have to drive like I am instructed to do by the company. I would appreciate it if you would stop yelling and I'm not going to accept any more name calling. I have a transfer here if you want to take another bus."

The man got up and immediately got off the bus. When I got to the layover zone in downtown Los Angeles, there were officers from the Los Angeles Police Department, transit police, and bus supervisors all waiting for me. The man had got to a phone and reported that I had attacked him.

I explained that the man and I had a disagreement I felt like it was just a man-to-man thing and nothing serious. A few days later,

I was called to the manager's office and was confronted with A10-page report that the man had written to the company about the incident. He demanded that I be fired.

I had had a lot of incidents while driving the bus. I was fortunate because my manager always supported me. He understood that I drove some rough and dangerous routes. He was confident that I handled each situation with wisdom. He ignored most of the complaints against me. He was Italian, he had spent a lot of years working for the bus company and he was about to retire.

His replacement would be a black man who wanted to make a name for himself. He came to the job promising that he would do everything better and that he would make major improvements to the way the company was being run. He would handle each complaint differently. For him, the customer was always right. For me, it meant having to report to the office nearly every day to answer any complaint no matter how trivial. With him, I went from having no write-ups to being written up constantly.

Early one Sunday morning, a man who seemed to be having a bad day, became extremely angry when my bus pulled away from the curb in front of him. He was far enough behind for me to pull away safely and since there was no other traffic on the street, he could have moved over a lane without incident.

The man was angered to the extreme by the bus pulling out in front of him. He drove in front of the bus, waited until I picked up speed, then suddenly stopped. The accident that he deliberately caused injured several passengers and me. I suffered a back injury. It was the end of my bus driving career. I had grown tired anyway.

Maybe it was because I was driving the bus and always out in public that I was always experiencing these incidents but, I had encountered too many racist incidents in California. It did not matter what the reason was, I was tired.

Once again, I wanted to get away. To move someplace else. The Pacific Ocean was as far as I could go. The next time I moved, it would have to be to another country. I did not know what would be waiting for me in another country. Every place I moved to in the United States was more racist than the place I had left. What would I have to face beyond the ocean?

It was plain to see why there was so much blatant racism here. Whites always win. In any confrontation when another race is involved, the police always come to the aid of the white person. There was no such thing as a fair fight between men if a white man is involved. The white person calls the police. The police always have the advantage. They immediately take the side of the white person.

And whatever the person of the other race says is meaningless. The Rodney King case was the perfect example. Had it not been filmed; it would not have been believed by some. With the situation on film for all to see, the defense of the policemen was: "They feared for their lives."

Eventually one finds that "Protect and Serve" refers to whites, especially rich whites. While driving the bus, it was easy to see that it could be a big mistake driving through the neighborhood of the rich if you were not white, especially at night. (This did not mean that finding yourself in the wrong black neighborhood was not just as dangerous.)

When you hear stories like; a black gang member was wounded in a shootout with the police and the police came to the hospital, pulled a gun on the doctor and told him, "if you do not let this man die, we are going to kill you." You could wonder if the story was true at first. After living here, for a while, you find out that it was. In my encounters with the police, it seemed like evil was taken to a new level.

I did not know if I could stay out of trouble. I had not met one black or Latino who had not had some bad experience with the police. There was no place for me to go back to. As a Machine Gunner in the Marines, I was told that my job was one of the most dangerous a person could have. I could not see living in the south, in Detroit, Texas or California being any less dangerous.

One thing for sure, I had not lived in any city that I wanted to return to. I began to wonder if education was a means of escape. Education comes in many forms. I was taking a bus heading to California State University Los Angeles when I had the opportunity to talk to an old black lady I sat next to. I felt relaxed talking to her. She reminded me of my grandmother.

"Tell me young man do you read the Bible?"

"Yes ma'am."

"Do you see any difference and what goes on now and what went on in Sodom and Gomorrah?"

"Things are pretty bad... I don't know. I've seen so much that I wouldn't be surprised if God destroyed everything right now. I think we've Surpassed Sodom and Gomorrah."

"We have a merciful God. He gives us chance after chance to repent. Now people have become so arrogant that they feel like they are gods."

"That's true. Do you see the way people drive out here?"

"Well, there is a reason for everything. You see a long time ago that was segregation and whites always had to be first. If you went into the grocery store, you would have to wait for the whites before you could get waited on. In any office, government or otherwise, minorities were always overlooked while the whites were waited on. The result is, now you have a generation of people who don't understand why they should not be first in everything, even in traffic."

"That makes sense. Blacks and Latinos start wondering what is happening when they see people cutting them off, refusing to let them change lanes or pull away from the curb. After these things are done to them over and over, they start driving the same way, thinking that's the way you're supposed to drive, I guess."

The people who started this country never had any respect for other races. They labeled us minorities, and they don't plan to start respecting us now. This country is filled with evil. It's been like that ever since the white man landed here."

"Yeah, I've been looking for a way out. That's why I'm trying to go to school now. Not that I think education will help the situation. I just hope I can make enough money to move to a safe place, maybe one of those gated communities. It's funny, during slavery you could buy your freedom. I see slavery as something that has evolved now. Freedom is out of the question."

"God is the only way to freedom. You must trust Him. He'll help you find what you're looking for. Where we make our biggest mistake is, we think man is in control. We forget about God. God never created anything that he cannot control."

"I remember the words from the scriptures," I said. "Woe be unto them who put their faith in men."

CHAPTER 4

The Backside of the Bell Curve

In school I got lost in my studies, Just as I had during the seven years I trained in Taekwondo. With most of my time occupied with going back and forth to classes and studying when I was at home, the outside world seemed to disappear. At first, I was worried about being too old to go to school, but there were a few others there around my age.

When I found that (because of my service-connected disabilities) the Veterans Administration would help pay for my classes. I saw a counselor at the VA who would approve my application for me to get a degree in computer science.

The interesting thing about me being approved for courses in computer science was, I had spoken to a veteran's counselor about the same classes years before. I did not think it meant anything at the time, however, the counselor advised me to seek another field of study because blacks did not do too well in computer classes. Tests showed that I had an aptitude for investigation. I was excited because Sherlock Holmes had always been one of my heroes.

I took a course in Private Investigation, graduated with honors and became very good at investigating. Ironically, one of the first things that I investigated was: Why blacks did not do well in computer courses. My finding was, I had been lied to.

This time I expressed interest in becoming a computer programmer. The counselor claimed that he could not locate the code number for a computer programmer, so he wrote down the code number for a computer operator.

The difference was that a programming degree would take four years, while training for a computer operator took two years. By claiming he could not find the code number he would save the government from having to pay for the two extra years that it would take to get a programmer's degree.

At West Los Angeles college I did well in computer science classes, but I became obsessed with anthropology classes. Especially the studies in religion, magic and witchcraft. I began to realize that there was a big difference between studying to find employment and studying to obtain an education.

The classes in anthropology explained a lot about the earth, its development and the inhabitants of earth and their development. Religious studies were really eye opening. I began to understand the things that men believed and why they believe them. Studies in religion, magic and witchcraft were especially interesting. These courses explained man's thirst for power and things that they would do to obtain power.

More interesting than my studies in anthropology was my getting to know the teacher who was a Russian lady. It was enlightening to find that she was white but her ideas about life and the world differed so much from the white people in the United States that I began to look at everything differently. Sometimes when the teacher spoke you got a clear understanding that she did not like Americans their ideas, their way of life or their beliefs.

The one thing that really touched me was, her belief and feeling that everyone who was born on this earth was entitled to their portion of this earth and that no one had the right to own land or people. Her way of thinking, to me, corresponded to scriptures I had read stating; God separates nations by borders.

I was always confused about those who wanted to conquer other lands and other people. To my way of thinking, skin color never mattered or determined whether one was cursed or not. Not being satisfied with the land God had given and desiring the land of others and what the land of others had to offer, was a curse.

I was thrilled by my anthropology classes, and I liked the class in computer science. I liked learning about logic, numbers, computers, and how they work. In elementary school and High school, math was my hardest subject. I was amazed at how I had begun to understand numbers. I sometimes stayed at school 12 hours a day. I loved programming and working with computers. I also became fascinated with history and Spanish. I wanted to learn everything.

I was seated in a Spanish class waiting for the teacher, when a fellow computer science student walked by and saw me in the room. The man was from Africa.

"What class is this?"

"It's a Spanish class."

"Why are you taking Spanish? Are you going to do business in Spanish countries?"

"You know, I never thought about it. I just wanted to learn the language. I dated a Hispanic lady once when I was a bus driver. She could not speak much English and I could not speak Spanish. She and her family moved to New Mexico, but I really liked her. I always wanted to learn her language. I would also like to learn at least one African language."

"In the business world, most people speak French these days."

"Even in Africa?"

"Yes, a lot of people who do business there speak either French or English. We don't get a lot of black men from America coming to do business. Africa is one of the richest areas in the world now. We welcome our black brothers from the United States, but it looks like the few who come don't stay in business too long. They come, make their money, then leave."

"I can understand that. We don't have the type of greed that some others have. What you described is what I would like to do, make enough money to live comfortably and make sure my family lives comfortably then relax and enjoy the money that I have made. I think the people who try to grab all they can and try to become the richest men in the world, have mental problems. Eastern philosophy teaches, "a man is rich when he knows that he has enough." I'm not greedy."

"You know you're pretty sharp in computer programming. I can see why the whites tried so hard to keep you guys from getting educated. They are afraid that, if they had to compete fairly with you, they would lose everything."

"So, you know about the racism here then?"

"Of course, I do. At one time I was trying to work while I took my classes. After a few months, I was so stressed out by the racist treatment I received on the job, all I wanted to do was to get back home. That may not be the answer now though. The whites realize how rich Africa is, and now they want to take it over, like they took America from the Indians."

It was just like I feared. Leaving the country would probably be a mistake. Now I understand why the KKK always predicted a race war. Eventually black men in America would have to fight not just to be free, but to keep from being exterminated. There is no end to greed.

I don't think I ever wanted to leave school. However, soon it was time to graduate. It was a beautiful feeling. I thought I had accomplished something. I have my AA degree in computer science and a certificate in computer programming. Spoke a little Spanish and had done well in anthropology I was on the Dean's list and had graduated with distinction.

I had also come to know a lot about some of the other students. There is a backside to that book *"The Bell Curve."*

From the time that I was very young, I had been taught that whites are more intelligent than the other races. However, in school you find that whites struggle to learn just like everybody else. Sometimes classes are easier for whites than blacks because there is less stress at home.

It is no mistake that there are a lot of poor blacks, but the white supremacist makes sure that blacks are kept poor. It is harder for a person who does not have the proper food or clothing to put forth his best effort.

White students also usually have materials at home to help with schoolwork, like computers and other things that many minority children do not have access to.

In poor communities. There is gang violence, police brutality, noises from helicopters keeping you awake at night, and no place to relax and study. Still poor children have to attend classes and when their grades fall below those of the whites, they are called inferior.

You also become aware that white teachers often give breaks to white students that they do not give to others. In certain situations, blacks who get answers wrong on tests have to live with the grade. I have watched white students have grades changed by white teachers. I'm more than sure that they feel as if they are helping their race, just like the employers who place negative reports on the work records of blacks so that they can say whites are better.

More important than anything else, there's a lot of cheating on the test. Whites with money sometimes pay people to take tests for them. The answers to some tests are purchased and if you talk to some who have attended colleges or universities, you will find that sometimes members of fraternities and sororities sometimes managed to have the answers to tests.

Growing up thinking that I would never be able to attend college, I was so happy to have my degree that I wrote a letter of appreciation to the Department of Veterans Affairs. I had written to the wrong people.

I took my degree and my certificate and began looking for work. I was anxious to get into the computer field. I began getting the same answers each time I applied for a job. "You'll need a four-year degree to program computers. A two-year degree won't do. The Veterans Administration knows that."

I had to hear that statement a few dozen times before I realized that I needed more education to get into the computer field. I contacted the VA informing them that I needed a four-year degree to program computers.

I did not hear from the VA for a long time, so I began attending California State university myself. I intended to take classes in computer engineering, but I found I needed more math. There was, however, a class in advanced Taekwondo. I felt at home there.

There was a lot of tension in the air during this time. The Gulf War was about to start. Students were huddled around TV sets waiting to see if the country was going to war. I did not know what the war was about. Flyers were being passed around the school that said, "Bush, Thatcher, Kissinger and others are intent upon imposing what they call a new world order, in both continental Europe and the so-called third world."

Never liking to discuss politics, the only discussion I remember having about the war was in a locker room just after a Taekwondo class. The fighting had begun, and everyone seemed to be happy at the destruction being done to Iraq.

I remember a conversation with a guy from India, "you know it's hard for me to understand Americans. Everyone is so happy about the United States and these other big countries beating up on a little country like Iraq. It's just like a bunch of big bullies beating up on a helpless man, this is a weird place."

I was wondering how the black military men felt about being a part of a war that blacks probably should not be involved in. Their problems were with the United States.

Maybe whatever is played out on a large scale in the universe, is played out on a smaller scale among men. The black soldiers returning from the war came home to see what they had done to Iraq on a large scale, being done to Rodney King.

I had been given an appointment with the VA, and I was hoping that I could get some help to continue my schooling. When I arrived for the appointment, I found that I had to wait for over an hour before the counselor showed up. A very impolite man ordered me into his office. He looked over my files for a long while in silence then he sat back and frowned.

"You know, I think you have been to school enough. Education is not what you need. What you need is a damn job. Now, I'll tell you what I'm going to do. I'm going to put you in an employment program. They'll help you to find a job, but the only way that I'll approved that is, you'll have to submit to regular drug testing."

The longer he spoke, the angrier I became. It took all of the discipline I could muster to let him finish speaking, when he did, I was ready to fight.

"Listen, Mr. Anderson. There seems to be some kind of mistake here. I did not come here for your advice about whether or not I should increase my education. I applied to the VA for a training allowance. I think your job is to approve it if I'm eligible or to disapprove the application if I'm not. Now if you are telling me, you are denying my application, I want some written information on how to appeal your decision."

The counselor was taken off guard. I was starring him straight in the eyes. He began to sweat, then he got up and nervously began to look through his desk drawers.

"I don't have any appeal forms right now," he said.

"Then what do I do about my application?"

"OK, the meeting is over." Mr. Anderson went to the door and opened it to show me out.

I knew that there was something wrong with the way my case was being handled by this man. If I did not do something, no one would ever hear about the incident, I would lose my training allowance and Mr. Anderson would have successfully denied another black person what he was entitled to.

I left the office and went upstairs to the Disabled American Veterans office. I explained the incident to the man who now interviewed me. I did not think it would do a lot of good. I was sure that with him being white, he would cover for Mr. Anderson. He did not.

"You say the guy's name is Anderson? You know, usually he's one of the good ones."

"Maybe so, but what do I do about my application?"

"Well, the VA cannot deny an application without putting it in writing. Did he give you any paperwork?"

"I did request an appeal form. He did not give me one."

"Anytime the VA denies a claim, they have to put it in writing. If he didn't give you anything today, it will have to come through the mail. Wait until you receive the denial notice. Then we can fight him."

I felt that it was time to fight back now. It was too stressful thinking that taxes paid by me and my family go to pay racist policemen and government employees. Employees who use these government offices to do harm to as many blacks as they can.

I had decided to try every legal means that I could to get something done about what had happened. If I was unable to, Mr. Anderson will receive a personal visit from me in the parking lot after work. The gangster in me had reemerged.

I began to locate the addresses of the congressman, senators, anyone who had the power to correct the situation. No one answered. I decided to write President Clinton as a last resort.

I had suffered a lot of mental damage after I faced this man. I could no longer concentrate on my studies. I began to drop classes and my grades dropped. I could no longer study because thoughts of revenge from myself and for my race stood in the way. My first thoughts were to begin randomly killing whites like they used to bomb our churches in Alabama. I knew that thought came from Satan himself. Those actions would make me just like the people I hated.

I found that I was far too religious for that and that I did not know any white man who was worth going to hell for. Killing innocent people is what they do. The thought of becoming like them made me worry about myself. I began to pray and to ask forgiveness for allowing those kinds of thoughts to enter my mind. I came to the conclusion that whatever I did I would have to be able to justify it with my God.

When I began thinking like that, I realized, God was not involved. The thought of God not being with me was the most frightening thing that I could imagine. I began to consider the matter a personal one between Mr. Anderson and myself, if anyone was to be harmed, it would be the one who intentionally did harm to me. My rage had taken over. I was back to my original plan to wait for Mr. Anderson in the parking lot after work. To confront him man to man. Before I finish planning my actions, I received a response to my letter to President Clinton.

Because of my letter to President Clinton, the matter was looked into. I received a letter from the Director of the Veteran's Administration's Regional Office. I don't think I had smiled in about a year. However, when I saw how the director tried to cover up what had happened, I must have laughed for two days. Before, this man would have considered himself far too important for me to speak to. He had gone from feeling superior to lying, scheming, and covering up the racist activity of his office to try to make himself and the other racist seem like honest men. The scriptures say that God himself hates liars.

I felt good anticipating going back to school. It had been nearly a year since the incident with Mr. Anderson. I had become so tense during that year that I did not notice the tension that had gripped Los Angeles.

I had taken a bus from California State University, and I was transferring to a bus in downtown Los Angeles that would take me to West Los Angeles. I was at the bus stop across from the courthouse. A car was driving by that was in such bad shape that I, along with others at the bus stop, began to laugh.

The car could barely get to 25 mph. It had rust from end to end and smoke was coming from beneath the hood as well as the back of the car. There were four black people in the car, two women in the front seat, two men in back.

The driver attempted to stop for a red light, but the car kept creeping forward. Eventually, the car bumped into the car in front of it waiting for the light to change.

The driver of the car that had been bumped, immediately put the car in park and got out. The driver was a white female, a child was riding with her. She instructed the child to stay in the car, and angrily walked back to the smoking car.

"OK, you hit my car! Park this thing and give me your license and insurance information."

"Listen," replied the driver from the smoking car. "I barely touched your car, so I don't think there could be a lot of damage, so if we could exchange licenses and telephone numbers, I would take care of any damage. Please try to understand that we are driving this car because of an emergency. I cannot park and turn the engine off because it won't start up again and we really have to go."

"I don't care what kind of emergency you have. We have laws here, now park that car!"

The driver of the smoking car reached into her purse, presented her driver's license, and wrote down her telephone number. She tried to hand them to the driver of the other car, who refused to take them.

"I told you, you are not going anywhere. Now, park this car."

The driver of the smoking car tried to drive off. The other lady reached inside the car and attempted to grab the steering wheel. Someone in the back seat reached out and slapped the woman. She jumped back in shock. She looked around for witnesses. There were three Asians, five Latinos, and myself waiting at the bus stop.

The lady looked towards us and asked, "did you see that?" Everyone turned away from her. The smoking car drove off.

I was laughing at the incident when I got on the bus. I sat down near the back of the bus and pulled out a book. There was too much noise coming from the rear for me to concentrate. I look back into the faces of four young men dressed in what was referred to as gang attire. "What are you looking at?" One of the men asked.

I did not respond. I turned around, put my book away, and laid my head against the seat. I heard the same voice coming from the back. "I said, what are you looking at?" I did not answer.

"What's up with this long hair anyway? Who the fuck do you think you are, Michael Jackson?"

MILLION MAN MARCH

"Yeah, and what's up with them pants? Niggers don't wear pants that tight these days." Another one said. My pants were not tight, they just were not sagging.

I began to laugh. This seemed to disturb the young men.

"So, what the fuck are you laughing at? You see something funny?"

The bus was approaching my stop. I got up and walked towards the back door, close to where the men were sitting. As I stood at the door one of the men came closer.

"So what's up man? I'm talking to you, and you are ignoring me and laughing and shit." The bus was pulling up to my stop.

"I was just thinking, you guys are laughing at my pants, and I'm laughing at yours. They've got to be 5 sizes too big and hanging off your asses."

"Fuck you! You Michael Jackson hair wearing motherfucker."

"You guys are too young to know what's going on, I was wearing my hair like this long before Michael Jackson was born. And if I wanted to change the style of my hair or my clothes, it will not be because of what some stupid young punks say."

The smile left my face, and the young man who had walked up to me stepped back. The bus stopped and the door opened. "You guys take it easy." I said as I got off the bus.

I was thinking how good it was to get home, as I walked towards my apartment. That was so much tension in the air you could feel it. I did not think it was good to be outside.

When I got home, there was a commotion in the driveway. A van was blocking the parking space of a lady who lived in the building. The lady had just gotten home from work, the van was blocking her parking space and there was nowhere to park on the street. That was a Hispanic man standing by the van. "Why don't you move the van and let the lady park in her space?" I asked.

"I don't have the keys; my boss has the keys."

Didn't you tell him that the lady needs to park?"

"Yes, I told him. He says she can wait."

"Would you get him for me?" The man walked into one of their apartments and came back with a white man.

"Listen, this lady is just getting home from work and you're blocking her parking space."

"Look, I'm working in this building. I'll be through in about 20 or 30 minutes, she can wait."

"Why don't you just park somewhere else? There are other empty spaces here the tenants rent these parking spaces just like they rent the apartment."

"I don't have the keys. I work for the company that owns this building. It won't hurt for her to wait just a few minutes."

"I'll tell you what. I'm going to put this thing in neutral and push it out of the way."

The man ran towards the van "No! Don't touch that van."

"I'm going to move this van and I'm going to mop this parking lot with you if you try to stop me."

The man pulled out the keys and started the vehicle. The Hispanic man smiled and gave me a thumbs up.

I finally got inside my apartment. This has been one hell of a day. I thought. I turned on the TV. The police officers who had beaten Rodney King had been found not guilty. The Los Angeles rebellion of 1992 had begun.

The rebellion that occurred in 1992 is now referred to as the LA riots. This is because of a culture that has developed over a long period of time.

Culture was the topic of discussion in one class at school. The teacher asked that each student present a cultural speech, then she said something that surprised most of us.

"Now I know that the white students are going to come to me and say, "we don't have a culture." You can give this speech about some other culture or just do the best you can."

MILLION MAN MARCH

I talked to another student, an Asian lady who happened to be a schoolteacher. "Don't you think it's kind of funny that whites don't think that they have a culture?"

"I hadn't paid it any attention before, but now that I think about it, even in teachers' meetings, they always talk about other cultures, but when they refer to whites, they always say mainstream."

"You know what I think? It's not that they don't have a culture, they would rather keep their culture hidden because part of their culture is the abuse of other racist."

"Interesting.... I mean, some of the things you find out. Like I was doing a report on slavery, and I ran across this old history book. I thought that I would find a lot of information in there. I found one paragraph on slavery and one picture of an African man selling another African man into slavery."

"That is the way they want people to view slavery as blacks selling blacks. My God! If niggers are going to sell each other, What is a poor innocent white man to do?" We both laughed.

The day the speeches about culture were to begin was more surprising than the day the teacher had assigned them. Nearly every white student started his speech by stating that they did not have a culture or that their culture was education or teaching others. I began to wonder if they had been taught that by their parents or in all white schools.

I did not understand how people could feel as if they were born to educate or teach others until I watched a program on Geraldo. The guests were KKK members and skinheads. One of the guests told a Bible story that explained their mindset.

A young lady was doing the talking on Geraldo's show after a black man in the audience had made a remark about the Bible. One of the first statements that came that caught my attention was, "The Bible is not for black people anyway." Then she gave the white version of the creation. She said that God had created the colored races of people, but he looked and saw that they were not developing the land, so he created the white man to show them what to do. I could tell from the statements that, whites evidently had access to some information that others did not.

That story answered a lot of questions for me. If whites were taught this, they would automatically become racist. What choice would you have if you had been told that all the other races were stupid. If there is the belief that you were ordered to teach these stupid people by God, their belief that you should use whatever methods that work would naturally follow however, there is a big difference between teaching others and abusing others.

The culture that has developed is one of abusing any race that is not white. Some tribal people did believe that God had sent the white man to bring them technology, some even thought that white men were gods. After they saw their land being stolen, after they are introduced to poverty, homelessness, police brutality, racism, prejudice, and inhuman treatment, they become aware that this is the work of Satan. However, if you brutalize them enough physically and mentally, you can break some of them. (This is called civilization.)

Part of a white culture seemed to be finding and using cheap labor. They first tried to enslave Indians. That did not work out too well. It is said that the John Brown rebellion taught them that they could not enslave whites. Blacks were the cheapest labor for the cotton and sugar cane fields. Chinese where the cheapest labor for the railroads and the story goes on. The workers were not the ones who became rich. One thing for sure, the talk about being here to teach is a bunch of crap.

The main part of this culture is deceiving others about their culture. No one who believes in their God would accept white supremacy. People are forced into a lifestyle that they do not want.

Racism in the United States is not considered a problem but a way of life. Whites control the media so that only the stories that they want to get out are seen or heard by the public. Rule is by terrorism. Without constant police harassment and beatings, there would be continuous protest about the way the wealth of the country is distributed.

Racism was discussed in a psychology class at California State. Blacks and Latinos alike were anxious to discuss the subject so that they could find out about the things they had been told. As soon as the teacher mentioned the topic, several Latinos were anxious to tell what they had been told. "They say that we are rejects." The Hispanic students said. They wanted a response from the teacher, but they were ignored. In that class racism was spoken of as something that had occurred long ago in America's history. It was talked about as if it was nonexistent today.

The Rodney King beating, and the rebellion that followed, opened a new line of communication between people. People who met each other in public places began to talk about their experiences, only to find that many of the experiences were similar. Gangs that have been fighting for years began talking about a truce. People began to exchange information and knowledge over radio talk shows.

Black people began to share experiences that they had not talked about before. There was definitely a white culture. Abuse of other races was definitely a part of it. Making negative and untrue statements about other races to justify the abuse was also part of the culture.

Police officers were careful to keep using the words, "animal" and "monster" when speaking about Rodney King and the way he was acting. Then they began saying, "well, he was a fleeing felon." Somehow, the use of these negative statements and labels we're supposed to justify the beating.

It was hard for me to listen to a lady from Australia talk about the whites coming there and cutting off the heads of the men and placing the skulls around the women's necks. In addition, they would bury the babies in the soil up to their necks and kick the heads off. I wonder, what was the justification for that? Is that something God told them to do? Were they really listening to Satan, thinking he was God.

In 1839 Theodore Dwight Weld wrote,

> *"the slaves in the United states are treated with barbarous inhumanity… they are overworked, underfed, wretchedly clad and lodged, and have insufficient sleep… they are often made to wear round their necks iron collars armed with prongs, to drag heavy chains and weights at their feet while working in the field…, they are often kept confined in the stocks day and night 4 weeks together, made to wear gags in their mouths for hours or days, have some of their front teeth torn out or broken off, that they may be easily detected when they run away… they are frequently flogged with terrible severity, have red pepper rubbed into their lacerated flesh, and hot brim, spirits of turpentine, &c., poured over the gashes to increase the torture… they are often stripped naked, their backs and limbs cut with knives, bruised and mangled by scores and hundreds of blows with the paddle, and terribly torn by the claws of cats, drawn over them by their tormentors."*

The abuse of our people continues to this day. Physical abuse, mental abuse, torture, and terrorism have been recognized by our oppresses as their only way to dominate.

Books like *"The Bell Curve"* are published without the mention of a demonic type of mentality that seems to be connected to the claimed, superior intelligence.

CHAPTER 5

The Secret of the N-word

People who have some knowledge about racism recognize publications that seemed to be no more than attacks on black people. Most black people in the United States eventually find themselves under attack by whites. It is terrifying to a child to find that there are those who dedicate most of their lives to making life as miserable as they can for them and planning their deaths.

Shortly after I moved to California, I was talking to the cashier in a market about a movie she had recently seen on TV.

The movie was about the life of Doctor Martin Luther King. I was shocked, surprised, and saddened when the young lady said, "you know it's a shame what they put on television today. I know those people in the South went through a lot of hell, but there is no way they went through all the stuff they showed in that movie."

I could not respond. I could only shake my head. I had flashbacks about my childhood in Alabama. I began to see why the Jews worked so hard to keep memories of the Holocaust alive.

I have no pleasant memories of my childhood. In Montgomery AL, the air was so full of hate and violence that I can never remember the sun shining. I must have been just old enough to understand words when I began to hear about men being lynched for looking at or whistling at white women.

When my mother would take me shopping, most of the white people you passed on the street would shout out "NI GG ER," some would rather spit on you. A lot of the places we passed had signs that read "whites only," if you had to be waited on by white cashier, no matter where you were in line, you would have to wait until all the whites were served. Then the cashier would have some way of disrespecting you, as if they wanted to be sure you knew that they hated you.

As a child I could only wonder how people who do not know you can harvest so much hate. White children just old enough to speak could say the word "nigger" when a black person passed.

Whites refused to use the same water fountains or toilets as minorities. There were two of everything, but they were different. The things reserved for whites only were usually expensive and well-kept while they used the cheapest material available to build anything that was for minorities. Black toilets and water fountains were always out of order and whites would say that "blacks don't need anything because they'll only destroy it anyway."

Tax money went for the comfort of the whites, with as little money as possible used for blacks. Whites would say that blacks were used to living in trees anyway, so we did not need anything.

I began working in a grocery store as soon as I was old enough. I quickly found out that store owners would make sure all the best products went to markets in white neighborhoods. Products that were defective or outdated would be the only things available for blacks, at inflated prices.

The man who owned the store where I worked, had a deal with the railroad to pick up merchandise that had been damaged while being delivered on the trains. Products that would have otherwise been trashed would be given to the supermarket owner and he would place them in his markets for sale to blacks. Packages of food with broken seals, bent and punctured cans, contaminated meats, outdated milk, and products that were not supposed to be sold at all, were sold to blacks at inflated prices.

The best products went to white neighborhoods at reduced prices because the profit had been made off blacks. Blacks did not have the option of shopping at other stores because they had signs that read "white only," and a black person could lose his life entering one of these places.

In places that were not labeled "white only," minorites were required to enter through the back door and sit in the back. Things got even scarier when a lady named Ms. Rosa Parks, refused to give up her seat on a bus for a white man. After that incident whites became even more vicious.

Blacks boycotted the buses. I can remember listening at the bedroom door of my grandmother's house, to the people holding what they called a "mass meeting." Blacks would get together at each other 's homes to plan ways to travel without using the buses. Everyone had to be careful. If the whites found out where the meetings were being held, more than likely the place would be bombed or there would be drive by shootings.

My mother was young and unwed. We lived in the projects. The projects were where poor blacks lived. My mother never got welfare (She worked cleaning white people's homes), but a lot of people in the neighborhood did.

The people who were on welfare got barely enough money to survive and the government spent millions of dollars spying on them to try to find a reason to stop the payments. Welfare people would be sneaking around homes at night, peeking through windows, questioning neighbors, and making surprise late night visits.

If a woman had a man in the apartment, it was grounds to stop her payments. If the furniture was too nice, or if she received a gift from someone, the payments would stop. Everyone had to be constantly on the lookout for these welfare people.

MILLION MAN MARCH

Welfare recipients got a lot more stress than assistance. The projects were overflowing with hungry children. The food that they were able to purchase with the small amounts of money they received had to be rationed. Most of the apartments in the project had locks on the refrigerators so that the children could not eat between meals. It was crucial to make the food last from one check to another.

Whites hated the idea of giving blacks anything. Whites would complain that we were too lazy to work and did not deserve welfare at all. They would call the people without jobs "lazy," and the ones who worked were paid as little as possible. Skill and education meant nothing and when there was a lot of racial tension, like there was when miss Rosa Parks refused to give up her seat, the working people began receiving more abuse on the jobs. People were also attacked going to and from work period.

As children we had nothing and expected nothing. We did not have much of a life expectancy and no one really wanted to stay here. The most terrifying thought of all was to have to grow up and go through what our parents were going through at the hands of whites.

I lost my job at the market when some college students spotted the store owner and some other men dressed in policemen's uniforms on horseback, beating up on blacks during the marches. The owner swore that he was not one of the men, but there were too many witnesses. The college students began picketing the store until it went out of business.

There was nothing to do in the projects and no one had any money for recreation, so boys usually just hung out on the corners. At first, we did not call ourselves gangs, but whites did. A lot of guys got in trouble for stealing. It was easy to start stealing because most of the guys were hungry. It was better to steal from someone else than to break into the refrigerator at home.

We learned early in life that the educational system was flawed. The schools were segregated, and a lot of teachers would constantly tell us how we must improve to be accepted by the white people.

Some blacks were made to feel bad about being black. Among the gang members, there was black pride. We considered ourselves more manly than white men. We began calling each other "Nigger."

To us, the word meant the opposite of white. Among the gang members "Nigger" was never a term of disrespect. There were those who wished to be white, but many of us were perfectly satisfied being who we were. It did not matter that we were poor, and it did not even matter that we were called Inferior. The only time that we had problems was when we had to interact with whites.

We knew that whites called us all niggers. The word coming from the mouth of a white person always has and always will be an insult because whites created the word to be an insulting word. We had heard about the popular song about Hawaiians, "You may call them Hawaiians, but they look like niggers to me." We knew that Indians were referred to as "red skin niggers" and Arabs were called "niggers with sheets."

With all of the hate directed towards them, we could not understand why parents still tried their best to get along with whites. The more the blacks wanted peace, the more combat they got from whites.

The younger generation wanted a change. A war would have been alright with us; we were being killed anyway. Police beatings like the one seen in the Rodney King incident went on every day. Lynching was entertainment for whites.

When the young men got together, we would exchange stories about police encounters. Police would stop you for nothing, then ask some stupid question like, "do you like my wife, nigger?" If you answered yes, it was grounds for a beating. If you answered no, it was grounds for a beating.

Some would be asked to spread out on the hot hood of a car and would be beaten when they moved because they could not stand the heat. During the time of the bus boycott, a young black man caught alone at night might never be heard from again.

The Rodney King incident awakened in me the memory of being surrounded by a bunch of yelling, angry whites with death in their eyes.

Dr. Martin Luther King would take off his jacket, roll up his sleeves, and walk through the projects singing. We began to follow and listen to his speeches; the crowds grew bigger and bigger. I witnessed the birth of the civil rights movement.

I followed Dr. King as much as my mother would allow me. I had to miss one March because my grandmother needed me to pay a utility bill for her.

I walked towards downtown Montgomery noticing that the streets were completely empty. That was a dead silence until I got near the First Baptist Church. The church was filled with people and surrounded by police. The police were threatening to kill anyone who left the church.

The police guarding the church paid little attention to me as I walked by. About a block away, some other policemen were gathered on the corner with some white civilians. They were talking loudly about "killing all the niggers in the church." I wanted desperately to turn around, but I knew I had to pay my grandmother's bill.

As I approached the crowd of whites, the conversation about killing niggers got louder. They wanted to make sure I heard their words. When I got closer and tried to pass on the sidewalk, the policeman pulled their guns, pointed them towards me, and everyone moved out to block the sidewalk.

The yelling was demonic. I tried to keep my head down so as not to look directly at anyone. As I made an attempt to go around, they continued to come towards me yelling nigger! They continued to block me moving out into the street until I was all the way out in the middle of the street. I kept walking, moving farther out into the street as they moved out to block me. I thank God that I got by alive.

Doctor King was strictly nonviolent. He always told us that the marches would be peaceful. The more peaceful the marchers got, the more violent the police got. They would ride through the crowds of demonstrators beating people on the heads with their clubs. They use attack dogs and water hoses. We were always told not to fight back.

The boys around my age were willing to fight. Somehow standing still and taking abuse never seemed right to us. If Dr. King was going to stick to his nonviolent methods, we would seek out other leaders.

A group called the Black Muslims had begun holding meetings. Those people were not nonviolent and just the mention of them caused fear in both blacks and whites.

Until that time the only meaning FBI had to us was a movie on TV. When we inquired about the Muslims, blacks would warn us that if we got involved with the group, the FBI would investigate us. "Besides, we were told, they preach hate."

We found the meeting place and started attending. The groups were always small, and the speaker never got to talk without some kind of interruption. The older men told us that the FBI was going through a lot of trouble to keep blacks away from the Muslim groups. They would plant men in each of the meetings to create disturbances.

While the speaker gave the message, black men hired by the FBI would stand up and yell out obscenities until the speeches were interrupted. Security personnel would ask the man to leave, and fights would start. After seeing these struggles over and over, a lot of people who would have become members never came back.

MILLION MAN MARCH

We were much too young to understand then why they were so interested in keeping black people away from the Muslims. Both groups wanted equal rights for blacks. However, they did not care how many people followed Dr. King.

It is important that the term <u>equal rights</u> be remembered because that is what most of the demonstrators marched for during the civil rights movement. We grew up hating whites simply because they hated us. Almost none of the young people wanted integration. We wanted equal pay for equal work and equal opportunities. All that came from the movement was "integration", something that we were not interested in.

Integration opened the door to more white abuse and nearly destroyed black unity. Blacks could now go into places where they could not before and be called nigger from new locations.

I could never come up with a reason for being born. I along with others my age, thought that God had made some kind of mistake putting us here. We did not want to spend our lives fighting white people, not knowing what we were fighting for in the first place.

You can never get used to the people growing up around you being killed or imprisoned, knowing at any time, you could be next. Yet, we had to deal with that. When I got the opportunity to visit a courtroom, life in America became even more frightening. Young black men were being arrested in large numbers for nothing. They would be charged with felonies, then told by public defenders that the best thing to do was to plea bargain for a lighter sentence. That way, they were always guilty whether they had committed a crime or not.

We were told, "in the future, you niggers Won't have to worry about the KKK in white robes. It'll be the ones in the black robes doing the job." By Klansmen in black robes, they meant judges.

I was desperately looking for a way out. There was a war going on in Vietnam and they were looking for volunteers. I felt it would be better to die in a war with honor, than to be beaten to death or lynched by a bunch of crazy white people or black gangs. I volunteered for the United States Marine Corps.

CHAPTER 6

An Indigenous Man's Prayer

The thought of judges becoming klan members or vice versa did not bother us too much since we already thought that they were Klansmen all of the time. In Alabama, the klan, the Police Department, and the average white citizen were all the same to us. It did not matter what they labeled themselves. The only friendly white faces we ever saw were those who came to March along with us.

The KKK is much more prevalent in California than in Alabama. However, you could probably travel over this whole country and find KKK on the walls of public restrooms in every state. In Alabama we grew up thinking these were people who had an uncontrollable hate for blacks. We learned in school that KKK members wear the sheets because the organization had begun during slavery. Knowing that blacks feared ghosts, the sheets were first used to make them look like ghosts.

I had moved away from Alabama before I learned that Hispanics and Jews were also on the hated list. While driving the bus I heard a lot of stories about KKK activity from Latinos. Several people on different occasions have told me that ex police chief Darryl Gates was rumored to frequent klan meetings. There were also rumors about ex-DA Ira Reiner. Those of us who grew up in the segregated

South can recognize one on site, or by listening to their speech. The Rodney King beating was a classic KKK beating.

Although these beatings have been going on for over 400 years, with most of the white citizens being aware of that fact, the Rodney King video gave the whole world the true image of the white man. Billions of dollars have been spent to destroy the image of the black man, but here you see an undeniable representative sample of those who are supposed to be some of the country's finest white men in one of the most cowardly acts ever filmed.

The TV stations began to work quickly to protect these white men. We began to see thousands of white faces on the TV screen making excuses for these men. Each one trying to make a statement to justify the beating. The only white face I heard mentioning the word cowards was the police chief. Others came up with a lot of excuses, but their excuses only gave those who saw them a better understanding of how white supremacy works.

A white man saying that this was not a racial beating would only anger people more. They needed a black face to stand up and tell the public that the beating was not racial. They quickly got a man named Nate Holden to do this.

Despite authorities not wanting to charge any of these men with a crime, two of the men ended up on trial. These men were to be sacrificed to calm the public. The states criminal justice system would make sure that they did not serve any time. The federal government would later be bringing charges against these men.

The state would use one of the judges the whites in Alabama had told us about long ago. (KKK in black robes.) They held the trial in White City, they hand-picked a jury that they knew would let them get off, and some of the law enforcement officers began to lie on the witness stand.

The whole trial was to deceive the public (the world). Whites knew that the man would be released before the trial began. Blacks and Hispanics were looking at a different situation. If these men were set free, every beating black people had taken since slavery would have been OK and given approval by the justice system to be continued. Blacks had no choice but to rebel when the men were released.

The rebellion also gave the public a good look at how the system operates. The LAPD, though comfortable beating Rodney King when the odds were over 20 to one, quickly turned and ran when the odds were a little more even. Citizens were complaining about being unprotected, and it was learned that the policeman had backed down from a similar situation years before.

When the national guards arrived, black and Hispanic neighborhoods were locked up like prison cells. Large concrete blocks sealed off the streets and freeway entrances. The people could be shot like fish in a barrel. Minorities without realizing it, are just as much on reservations as the Indians, and someone has been doing a lot of planning on how to kill us all.

After the riots, everywhere I went, blacks and whites alike were making jokes about policemen retreating. Over the years the white supremacist has maintained strict control over the radio and TV Airways. They plan for the image of black men always to be negative. The Rodney King video gave the world the true image of the white man.

That had to be corrected. "Truth" is the greatest enemy of the people who are in power. It is written that Jesus Christ said: "Do not suppose then I came to bring peace to the world. I did not come to bring peace but a sword." That sword is called "truth".

Altering the truth was one of the greatest sins for Africans and indigenous Americans. Those who believe in God know that God cannot be fooled. The same people would have no reason to deceive anyone. In this culture, altering the truth is considered a skill.

Politicians, government officials, and businessman use professional liars they sometimes call "spin doctors."

On the TV stations, thousands of interviews were done with whites joking about the stupid blacks and Hispanics burning their own neighborhoods. Evil had won the day it seemed. The policeman had been freed, the jury members were appearing on talk shows pretending to be honest people, and the only people suffering were "the stupid blacks and Hispanics who burned their own neighborhood."

The police began arresting people they call "looters." Rewards were offered and poor people desperate for money began to turn each other in.

So many people were arrested as looters that some of them would have to be released because the law would only allow a person to be held for 72 hours before being booked, the whites would have considered releasing these people a defeat. Overnight the laws were being changed so that the so-called "looters" could be held longer.

Later, as a result of the riots, another trial was held. This time it was for the Reginald Denny beating. People quickly began to see the difference in the way the two cases were handled. Whites use the argument that the beatings were different because the other men were police officers.

Again, they had to call on one of the klan judges. This time to convict blacks, and this time it was more apparent how the system worked. They had to pass over a black judge for this case to get the one they wanted. Looking back over the trial of the policeman and a result, we can now see why the judge was picked. Later the same policeman from the Rodney King case were brought up on federal charges and were given unusually light sentences.

In the case of the Reginald Denny beating, they had to lie to the public as to why the black judge was passed over. The black judge (Judge Dorn) called in on a radio talk show and told what actually happened. Black people with no common sense can no longer fool themselves. We are under the domination of liars and crooks, and our taxes pay the salaries of the people who abuse us.

One of the men arrested after Reginald Denny beating was said to have been caught on film. During the trial close-ups of the man committing the act showed a man with considerable spaces between his teeth. The man on trial clearly did not. If there had been any honesty or fairness, the man should have been released as soon as the fact was revealed. For us old timers, the situation brought back memories of our youth. When a crime was said to have been committed by a black man, all black men would warn each other to get off the streets.

Law enforcement did not care if they had the right person, any black man could be accused, arrested and made to pay. (A book called "Hold Back the Night" tells the true story about a young black man who was arrested, had his fingernails pulled out, made to sit on hot coals and had his genitals cut off in order to make him confess to a crime that he did not commit, then he was lynched.)

As enhanced images of a spot on the man's arm was made to look like a tattoo on the arm of the man on trial. Those who know about the computer images know that they could have made the spot look like anything they wanted to.

The white majority wanted these men convicted, no matter what and who they were. A black female jury member appeared on a talk show later and actually said that she was doubtful about the man's guilt yet, she went along with the others.

Men began preparing for war. Black men would stop me on the street and ask if I needed guns or ammo. People would call in to radio station talk shows to report that policeman were out in white neighborhoods selling guns and warning people about situations in which the police might not be able to help them. In black neighborhoods, they were trying to talk the people into getting rid of their guns.

When things began to calm down, blacks found that a new spirit of black unity had been born. People who never spoke before began to talk. Gang members stop fighting each other. The gang leaders said that they had been shown without a doubt who the real enemy was. Radio talk shows were created in which blacks could exchange ideas and experiences some people began to get a real education and to look for solutions.

I had always felt that it would take a war to end white supremacy in America. Blacks would be out gunned and outnumbered, but it was still better to do the fighting than to be killed by bunch of heavily armed cowards or to be beaten to the death for recreation.

My problem was that my religion made me feel guilty about killing. After seeing how policemen get up on the stand place their hands on the Bible, swear before God to tell the truth and then lie on camera before God and man, it leads one to believe that these people really have power, but it can only be called demonic power.

Black men will never be able to live in peace under white supremacist domination. The reason for the domination in the first place is greed. Greed only increases, so no matter how little you have, eventually they'll want it. The key to dominating others lies in controlling weapons and wealth. They will never voluntarily give up either. Those who think that they will eventually receive equal treatment had better take a close look at the indigenous people here.

Most of the indigenous people were given the choice to accept the white culture or die. Many died because they could not or would not accept the culture that they were being forced into. It means turning your back on God and going along with dishonest politicians, federal agents, policemen, judges and lawyers. It means overlooking the fact that the government's main purpose is the domination of minorities by whites, if not, there will never have been a **Department of Minority Population Control.**

If the population of minorities is being controlled in a country where the majority always wins, it means that the minorities in this country will always lose. The so-called black leader's solution to the problem is the vote. With the population being controlled, a vote is a waste of time.

I can never forget a news report I heard on the TV that went, "by the year 2000 there will be no majority in the state of California because the Latino population will have outgrown the whites." This is called witchcraft.

To me that was like telling minorities to their faces, "you'll never win." Shortly after that report, we started to hear about California's Proposition 187.

Unlike the indigenous people, blacks try the best to fit in and find that they are unwanted. Some indigenous people had the choice of going back to the reservation where much of their culture is still intact. Descendants of slaves never had that option.

There was never an attempt by white Americans to live in peace and harmony with other races. Only attempts to control them and live in separate neighborhoods. When people are taken away from their culture, problems arise.

Whites must have done extensive experimentation in torture, abuse, and mind control. A documentary on early Americans shows a white man making the statement "if you take an Indian completely away from his culture, put shoes on him and cut his hair, he will become a white man." A lot of Indians suffered greatly and died because of these experiments.

There are those who feel that the country has progressed greatly since the whites took control. Many African Americans no longer think about how their lives might have been before slavery. They have been fooled into thinking that things are better here.

The children of the slaves have nothing to compare with this life too. Instead of trying to learn about their culture, they still carry hopes of one day being like their captors, never realizing they are trying to become part of a culture that has brought down Wrath of God and soon will have to face God's vengeance.

Life for some people in this country has been more of a Horror Story than anything else. Those of us who have experienced and lived through these horrors often wonder about God and question God's Involvement in the situation. In my youth, I accepted what I was told about myself. That as a black man I was cursed by God, that I was inferior. I no longer feel that way. Knowledge of God is a matter of seeking knowledge of God.

Before white man came to this country. Indigenous people were aware that that was an evil force. Whether they called it Satan or not, they knew that it was known as the liar, the deceiver, the accuser, and the author of confusion. These were things associated with evil.

There were also attributes associated with good people. Some stories about Columbus talk about his visit to a place that was like paradise. The "conquest of paradise" (a story about what followed after Columbus landed) is seen in what is called colonization. Indigenous people had an awareness of God just as they had an awareness of Satan and of evil.

The first indication that an evil force has come to this country was the lie that there was an intent to bring the knowledge of the one true God to people who were already aware of God. Indigenous people were confronted by people who used the lie as the tool. This was proof that there was more of an association by these people with Satan, than with God.

Having lived all of my life with those who have all the attributes of Satan, my <u>studies in anthropology open my eyes to truths that I was never aware of.</u> I was never more enlightened and spiritually moved than when I heard a prayer that was shown in a documentary about indigenous people in an anthropology class.

The indigenous man's prayer went something like this:

> *"As I look at the rising of the morning sun, I hope that I walk in peace. I hope that my family and friends walk in peace. I hope that my cattle walk in peace. I hope that the white man walks in peace, <u>back to wherever he came from.</u>"*

CHAPTER 7

Atonement

The 1992 rebellion had left so much destruction that a lot of familiar places were unrecognizable. A lot of places that I had frequented were no longer in existence. The Barber shop I went to was gone, the bakery, the health food store were all destroyed.

There was talk about rebuilding and a lot more laughter about people burning their own neighborhoods. Some black people had experienced two rebellions in Los Angeles. Reports show that as far as police brutality was concerned, not much had changed since the first rebellion.

The more educated I became while attending school, the more depressed I became. While riding the bus each day, looking at blocks and blocks of destroyed property, I began having the same thoughts I had growing up in Alabama.

What am I doing here? Is there really a God? If there is, why does evil seem to be winning? Does God mean for us to rebel against our oppressors? Why are young healthy black and Latino men being killed, beaten and imprisoned daily in a white culture when they would be happy productive citizens in their own culture? The problem was clear. The problem is white supremacy. What is the solution to the problem?

God has ways of making himself known to those who believe. It was not long before the laughter about blacks and Latinos burning their own neighborhood stopped. Some of the whites who were laughing at the fires found themselves having to deal with fire.

In 1993 God set his own fires. Some were referred to as the Malibu fires. In Malibu it was reported that 268 homes were burned. It was sad that some of the homes had such large stockpiles of weapons and ammunition that the firemen could not go near them.

More fires followed, then heavy rains and mud slides, with Homes falling from heels. Poor neighborhoods were not impacted by the disasters, all that are well to do. For some of us, God was letting us know that he was still in charge. It is written, "don't be concerned about what people do, watch how they end up."

There was still a lot of work to be done to rebuild the image of the white man after the Rodney King beating. The media began praising the firemen and a monument was built to honor them. In one interview with the news reporter, one man said; "I really do not understand the purpose of building a monument when most of the time all they could do was stand there and watch the homes burn."

It was on a talk show called "Front Page", hosted by Mr. Carl Nelson, that I heard about the stockpiles of weapons and ammo. It was on the same program that I learned about the Million Man March.

As I get older and look back at my life. I realized that all my father saw in his life was white oppression. When I die, all I would be leaving my children would be more white oppression. The country we live in as a whole, has long surpassed Sodom and Gomorrah and evil deeds.

Black people have absolutely no political power that cannot be taken by whites at will; it is well known that the rights of minorities are routinely violated. We have to fight racism on every job, in government, even in restaurants. No one escapes. Black men who guard the president found themselves the victim of racism in a Denny's restaurant one news story reported. Blacks who work in law enforcement experience bias from the people they work with. While they are helping them destroy their own race.

Their stories about black police officers and plainclothes being killed all wounded by white police officers. My heart sunk, when a black lady called in to a talk show and said: "our men are dying in the streets like cowards..." After a Los Angeles police officer shot a tow truck driver in the back. Black men did not agree with what the lady said because they do not want to be referred to as cowards.

Black men were programmed to be cowards during slavery. The methods of a white slave owner named Willie Lynch (and others) were used to cause serious mental damage to the slaves and their ancestors. Blacks do not have a chance of regaining their manhood until the damage is corrected.

Some black people today refuse to even read the "Willie Lynch Letter" and will try to deny their connection to slavery when, the people who were able to survive slavery are superior people. The very fact that we did survive is more than enough proof that there is a God and that we have had supernatural protection from the beginning.

With new lines of communication opening among blacks, people began to realize that many of our experiences were the same and if we were going to survive, we had to come up with solutions to our problems. Some black People were now ready for action and the idea of a Million Man March was a way to make a statement.

I realized that to reach my age was a blessing from God. I also realized that most of the black men who were born around the same time as I, did not make it, black men were still dying senselessly the way they were when I was growing up, and after I die millions of black men will come into this world and be killed before they get anywhere near my age.

I had marched for freedom in the 60s, yet I felt less than a man thinking about the world I was leaving for the black men who come after me. If anyone examined my life, what would they find. Saying; "I worked hard all my life." Is very close to saying; "I have been a fool all of my life."

I felt like our whole race was insulted by a Jewish man in a conversation held on a radio talk show. "I think it's senseless burning down your own neighborhoods." The Jewish man said. A black man responded. "I don't understand how you can say that when you have a Jewish defense league to defend your people."

"Yes, but you guys are Christians. You are supposed to turn the other cheek."

The first time I heard about the Million Man March, I knew that I had to participate. I felt that my presence would show that l, at least, disagree with the evil conditions that my people encounter in this country and that, I am willing to call it out.

With the conditions we live in, it is more of an insult to be called an African American than it is to be called a nigger. There is no sense in saying that the answer to our problems is the vote when voting has not solved anything so far.

When we see people actively making attempts to interfere with voting rights, most of the time all we can do is talk about it. The answer to our problems can be found in the same words that Moses spoke in the Bible: "let the people go."

There have always been attempts to destroy the image of strong black men. (Jesse Owens, Jack Johnson...) Having been trained as an investigator I am well aware that, without firsthand knowledge, we have to be very careful about saying anyone is guilty of anything. (Especially in a country where a young man can be forced to sit on burning coal and have his genitals cut off in order to make him confess to a crime that he did not commit.)

As a trained investigator and, a man who knows that I can be wrong, I can honestly say that; I do not know if O.J. Simpson or Michael Jackson were guilty but I do know that there was a lot of effort put into making the public believe that they were and, especially in the case of O.J., a lot of people will get real angry if you do not agree with them.

The philosophy that prevails in my way of thinking conforms to an eastern quote that says: "not everyone agrees that every idea is right but, everyone surely thinks that his own ideas are right."

Too many court cases turn out to be nothing more than performances for the public. Police killings of unarmed men running for their lives are nothing more than a continuation of lynchings that have gone on for too many years. Policemen have organizations that will proclaim their innocence no matter what the situation and many get a paid vacation after the killings. (Job suspended with pay.)

I began to get information about the Million Man March by listening to talk shows and talking to men on the street inquiring about their feelings on the March. The more men I talked to the more afraid I became.

There were more negative comments about the March than positive. Some say it it would be too easy for the whites to ambush and kill a bunch of us at one time. Others said that they could see no reason for a March. Others said marching was a thing of the past. Others felt like they had been "good little niggers" and had nothing to atone for.

On October 13th, 1995, an article written by a prominent black man in Los Angeles was published. The title was: Why I won't be in Washington on Monday." In his article he stated, "I, like millions of other African American men, have no reason to atone for anything. I Attended a black college, hosted a black radio talk show, and ran for a seat on the Los Angeles City Council. Married to a black woman and working to curb gang and youth violence, I challenge this litmus test, to the notion of taking a day off from a job simply to draw attention to the problems facing black men in this country."

I was angered by this black man's article. For me, he was a prime example of the weak and cowardly black males that had been created by slavery. Our forefathers in Africa had nothing to atone for when many of them were kidnapped and brought here as slaves. During slavery black men had nothing to atone for when their women were raped, their children taken and sold, the men beaten, brutalized, tortured and forced into labor. The slave masters worked hard to produce men like this prominent black man of L.A. They would be very proud.

Strong black men recognized the fact that something was wrong, they rebelled and kept trying to escape. It was the slaves like this modern-day black man who felt that the best way to survive was to continue working like "good little niggers" and to wait on the Lord. It was the strong man who would die to be free who ultimately moved the world.

He stated later in his article that many black men (like himself) we're no longer willing to be their brother's keepers. He failed to realize that men like him were the reasons that beatings like the one seen on the Rodney King video have continued from slavery to the present. When a black man is attacked, he knows he can never expect help from his brothers. This man did not seem to know that his attitude had been beaten into him and had replaced his manhood. The call was for a million men. I felt like the writer of the article did not qualify anyway.

Men who consider themselves God's creation have no choice but to follow God's rules, which includes being our brothers' keepers. That was the main reason we needed a day of atonement. Before our capture by whites, our God always came first. Too many black men have become satisfied with the fact that whites have placed themselves between us and God.

When men have become as brainwashed as the writer of the article, it is impossible to convince them that being a "good little nigger" will not stop white abuse. Blacks have gang problems, drug problems, and problems with fatherless children, but blacks have no power over their destiny here. Our lives have been designed by white supremacy.

Whites are pleased with people like the writer of this article. He is proof that some people can be successfully controlled. If they wanted to find him, whites would know that, he would be on his job. That is the reason he was brought here. His taxes pay whites to dominate him. Mr. Ross is a free man, as long as he does not resist white domination.

One out of three black men are in the criminal justice system, not because they are criminals. They are there because whites have planned for them to be there. A large number of black men are in the criminal justice system because of drugs. Whites define as illegal drugs. The use of marijuana by indigenous people can we trace back thousands of years and God definitely created it along with the rest of the plants. It took white supremacy to criminalize it. Whites can use alcohol (a man-made drug) and their religious ceremonies and criminalize the use of peyote in the religious practices of indigenous people.

There are constant negative reports on minorities who sell drugs in their neighborhoods without mentioning the fact that some drugs are believed to come from government agencies like the CIA. Some of the deadliest drugs like alcohol and cigarettes, are readily available, especially in minority communities. If our government is against drug use, why is it that you can look at news films of

MILLION MAN MARCH

American troops marching into places like Somalia, passing out free samples of cigarettes to the blacks there? Does the government work for the cigarette company? Or do the cigarette companies work for the government?

Without white domination, blacks have started successful towns like Allensworth in California. Whites sabotaged the town simply because the blacks were successful. There's also the case of "Black Wall Street" where whites had once again become disturbed by black success and bombed the place.

The blacks in Allensworth and the ones in the story of "Black Wall Street" had nothing to atone for. That did not stop them from being attacked.

The whites who control California today have the same mentality as those who once tried to put measures in their state charter to prevent free people of color from entering California, later they tried to enslave free blacks men. Today there have been renewed attempts to bring back slavery with a new spin.

I cannot fault the ones who refused to attend the Million Man March, but I wondered if they were being honest with themselves. Without self-rule, men cannot call themselves men. Whites control wealth, the weapons, the military, law enforcement, the court system, and the prison system.

With that type of control, just like in slavery, they can come into your home whenever they want, take away your wife and children, beat you, kill you, take away your wealth, and lie about what happened without recourse.

Every black man in America should have staged a protest after the Rodney King beating because Rodney King represented every black man in America and no honest person can deny that it was a racist attack. Had the black men today not been broken during slavery, the race war they speak about would have started with the release of the video. Because the methods of Willie Lynch are still in effect, a lot of black men feel as if what happened to Rodney King has nothing to do with them and that slavery is long gone from the mind of white America.

When we speak of evil men, we talk about people like Hitler, when in fact, there are other politicians and people in position of power who are more evil, dishonest, and sinister. We talk about black-on-black crime and how dangerous the gang members are when black men like Clarence Thomas have brought and will bring about the destruction of more black men than all the gangs combined there is no greater example of a useful slave than Clarence Thomas.

It is not difficult to see what is happening in this country. Big business is investing in prisons and the politicians are setting in motion the laws to make sure prisons are full and prisoners never get out. Slavery (with a new spin) has been reintroduced.

In the days leading up to the Million-Man March, I never ran into another man who said that he was attending the March. When I inquired as to how to sign up, I was directed to 4339 Degnan St. in Los Angeles. There I found a fairly long list of names. The addresses were from all over Los Angeles. Some homeless men had also signed.

I was instructed to appear in Washington on October 16th, 1995, at the capital. I was supplied with identification to show that I was part of the March and told that all I had to do was to be there. I could leave at any time. I had an uncle (through marriage) who lived in Washington. My plans were to fly there, have him pick me up at the airport, and stay at his house until the March. (It was after the event that I found that he was nervous about the March and wanted nothing to do with it. He did not tell me but would give me the run-a-round. I would be on my own.)

I was continuing to meet people who still came up with so many reasons not to go, I started to wonder if there would be only a few of us there from California. Some callers to the talk shows said that a low turnout was expected from California. I felt that I had to go, even if I found myself there alone.

I consider myself a hardworking, educated, law abiding person who respects women. Because I do not sell drugs or commit acts of violence against my brothers, I still could not convince myself that I have nothing to atone for.

All black men do not abuse women. However, just because some men have respect for black women does not mean that black women have respect for them. A lot of problems that exists between black men and black women come from a condition known as "survivor's guilt." Can any black woman who is a descendant of slaves really forgive black man for not accepting death instead of slavery? Can black men really forgive themselves?

There may be black men in America who have nothing to atone for, but these men moved to this country willingly. Many of us who are descendants of slaves feel that, if for no other reason, we should have atoned for not being men. If we did not need saving, the FBI would never have been worrying about "preventing the Rise of a black Messiah." Just like babies were killed during the time of Jesus.

There have been warnings all down through history about the dangers of not putting God first in our lives. For African Americans, it is our only hope for salvation. The problem is whites have placed themselves and their weapons between the black man and God. Whites control the weapons and the legal system. To defy white law means death, and since many of these laws are in conflict with God's laws, we cannot serve both.

Black Americans are in situations where if nothing is done about white supremacy our race soon will no longer exist. If something is done about white supremacy and we still do not put God first, our race will no longer exist.

CHAPTER 8

GOD first

Fear would prevent a lot of men from attending the Million-Man March. The reason given by most of the men that I talked to was that they were afraid that the government would set up an ambush and if the government did not do it, there were white militia groups who had started making threats.

I can remember a conversation with a young man a few days before I left.

"You know how this government works man. I think you guys would only be making it easy for them to kill a million of us at one time. I don't want to put myself in that position."

"Policemen kill black people in this country every day. You know for yourself that an innocent, unarmed black person can be beaten to death or blown away at any time by policeman in front of a whole neighborhood of people. The next day you see the media tell the whole world he drew a gun on the policeman.

I don't want to die like that. When I go to Washington, it won't be about fighting, but if the fight should start, I'll be ready. I believe that I could rest in peace if I die fighting back. Dying is not important, we are all going to die anyway. How you die is what matters."

MILLION MAN MARCH

I had to leave knowing that there was a chance that I would not be coming back. I was thinking, maybe we should have accepted death instead of slavery. Maybe this was our second chance.

I would take a bus to the airport. I never felt so alone as I did while walking through my neighborhood. The men who saw me leaving wished me luck.

At the airport I saw others who were going to the March. I was relieved to find that there would be others there. When we landed at Dulles airport, the number of black faces I saw arriving from everywhere in the country let me know that the March was going to be big.

It was Friday night when they arrived my uncle did not show up at the airport. When I called, he told me that he lived a pretty long way from the airport and that I should take a bus into DC. The bus was nearly filled with marchers.

As we approached DC, some of the passengers commented on the beauty of our nation's capital. Someone pointed out the Washington Monument, and there was talk about how nice it would be to walk around looking at the historic buildings and locations.

I got off the bus and went to a phone to call my uncle again. I got nervous when I used the pay phone because there were big cockroaches on the street. I was thinking, wow cockroaches, this close to the capital.

Later I found it amusing that I had become so used to seeing homeless people that I took more notice of the cockroaches near the pay phone than I did of the homeless people there.

I was on K St. only a few blocks from the capitol. Homeless people were everywhere. Some with their belongings in shopping carts. Some were asleep on park benches and others in doorways.

When I called my uncle again, an emergency had come up and he would not be able to pick me up that night. It was already past midnight. I would try to find a hotel room in the area.

I found most of the hotel rooms full. The rest were too expensive. I did not expect to have to rent a room and did not bring along enough money. I did not know the city and my feet were hurting after carrying my luggage from hotel to hotel.

I sat on a park bench to rest. Homeless people were asleep everywhere. I felt like one of them. The weather was nice, so I decided to sleep on the bench.

I had just closed my eyes when a homeless man walked up to me and asked for a quarter. "I'm in the same shape as you are." the man looked at me curiously.

"you're a fighter, aren't you?"

"Huh?"

"Don't you box?"

"No, I practice a little martial art, but---"

"Yeah, I knew you were a fighter. Come on give me a quarter man help a brother out."

"I wish I could. "

The man shook my hand and left.

I was about to close my eyes again. I jumped up when I saw a spider descending from a web in the tree next to the bench. It looked as if it was aiming for my head. I moved from one end of the bench to the other. Now I was afraid to close my eyes thinking I might get bitten.

I sat there looking at the street. There were a lot of young people out partying. Cars were filled with young women yelling at cars filled with young men and vice versa.

As the time passed, I saw fewer people on the street and more rats. The rats were out near the curb, but I was afraid of rats and was concerned that they might come closer if I fell asleep.

I began to feel stupid as I looked at the homeless people sleeping peacefully. There was no telling how many nights some of them had slept among the spiders and rats.

Later, policemen on motorcycles rode through the park. I was expecting them to ask the homeless people to leave. They did not. They looked around, then left.

My eyes were too tired to stay open now. I fell asleep for what must have been about 20 minutes. I was awakened that's something wet falling on my face. I opened my eyes to see that it had started to rain. It was coming down harder by the second.

The nearest shelter was the bus stop. I grabbed my luggage and ran to it. I sat there for a few minutes, shivering.

I began to walk. There was a taxi driver seated in his car drinking coffee. Approached and asked if he knew of a reasonable room that I could rent in the area.

"Go up to M St. If you go straight there from here, there's a hotel to your left and another to the right. They both are reasonable."

I thanked him and started walking. As soon as I got near M St. I saw beautiful a beautiful young lady in a short skirt flagging down passing cars. Walking in the street among the cars was another lady even prettier than the first. The women were prostitutes, and although it was raining, the street was filled with them.

Not far from the prostitutes were drug pushes. Some standing alone, others in small groups. The rain stopped for a while. More prostitutes and drug pushers appeared.

I had walked a long way in the direction the cab driver had told me to and never saw a hotel. I turned and tried the other direction. There was nothing that I could recognize as a hotel. My feet were hurting to the point where I was walking with a terrible limp. I sat at a bus stop to rest.

It started to rain again, I decided that the best thing to do was to go to the greyhound bus station and to place my bags in a locker. I started walking again. I asked for directions from an employee of the Holiday Inn that I passed downtown.

"Are you going to walk to the bus station?"

"Yes. All the rooms are filled. I got a lot of time to kill. And I really need to get rid of my bags."

"Yeah, but it is raining like hell, and that is no short distance. Do you know where First street is?"

"I don't know where anything is in Washington. I'm here for the Million Man March."

"Well, I still suggest you take a cab, but if you insist on walking, go down Massachusetts to 1st St. Massachusetts takes a turn somewhere down there, so be careful."

I was soaking wet and near exhaustion by that time. I thought I was being careful about staying on Massachusetts, but I found myself back on M street the neighborhood began to get more run down the farther I walked. I was surprised to see so much poverty so close to the capital. I was not surprised to find that, like in Los Angeles, blacks and Latinos live there.

I was limping along when a man seated on the stairs of a rundown apartment building call to me.

"Hey, what's up man?"

"how's it going? I replied.

"Are you here for the March?"

"Yes."

"Where are you staying?"

"What?"

"I said, where are you staying?"

I stopped and looked the man in the eyes. Analyzed him quickly. He was what I referred to as a hustler, probably on the lookout for out-of-town prey. The building served as a dope house and a place where the prostitutes took their clients.

"I'm looking for a place, do you know where any reasonable rooms are?" "Look. I can rent you a room. This is my place, and I can rent it to you cheap."

I did not think it was wise to go inside, but I wanted to learn as much as I could about what was going on. The building was so run down on the outside that I was curious about how it looked inside.

I was aware of what I had to be prepared for. Hustlers would sometimes pull weapons to rob people. If they thought you were weak, they might try to take your belongings, and sometimes a Coconspirator would be waiting behind the door to hit you on the head.

"How much are we talking about?

"Come on in, let me show it to you."

A big rat ran across the yard while we were talking, I limped up the stairs and put my luggage on the porch.

"No! Bring your bags with you."

This led me to believe that there would probably be a robbery attempt. When we entered the building, another rat ran across the hall.

The man introduced himself as CC. He led me up some stairs. We passed several rooms. Prostitutes were coming out of some of the rooms with their clients, others were going in.

CC opened the door to a room and showed me in. "Well, here it is how much do you think it's worth?"

I looked around. The only furniture was a mattress on the floor. Cockroaches crawled along the wall.

How much do you think it's worth, CC?

"I don't know. How much would you pay at the Holiday Inn or someplace like that?"

"The cheapest place I've found so far was the Days Inn. Their rooms were $110 a night. I only have $100."

"What do you think if I let you have this place for 20 bucks a night?"

"That's a good price. Unless I wake up tomorrow with my money and my luggage gone."

No one's going to bother you here man, especially a man coming here all the way from California just to March for us."

"Are you going to the March CC?"

"I can't."

"Do you know why we are here?"

"Yeah, you guys are marching for our rights."

"CC, believe me man. I have known brothers just like you in Alabama, in Detroit, and Texas, and in LA back in the 70s, I used to hustle myself. All I have left of that life now is my long hair. This long hair is probably the only difference between you and the man I used to be."

"You think you've been around?"

"I'm nearly 50 years old. I spent most of my young years going nowhere. Just like you, I'm lucky to be alive. Just like you, I'm lucky I'm not in prison. I had to learn to put the same energy I used in hustling, into trying to get an education. The more educated I became, the more the world changed. I did not get any richer, conditions did not get any better, but believe me things change when your attitude changes."

"If conditions did not get any better, what's the use?"

"Some men, men like I used to be, men like you are now, are only puppets on the string. Things get so hard that the only way you have to get over is crime. You think you will outlive the other hustlers, or avoid going to prison like the others, only to find out that you are all headed the same way, you just don't know it.

You think you are controlling your own life, never realizing that the road you walk has been built for you by white supremacy. Prisons are the fastest growing industry in this country. Believe me, your room is ready, it's just a matter of time before you get there. That's if you don't make it to the grave first."

"That's some heavy shit man."

"Think about it."

"What if I gave you the room for just $20 for as long as you want to stay?"

"That's OK." I could see that twenty dollars was important to him.

"Alright. If you don't find anything, I'll hold the room for you if you leave me $10."

"No thanks."

When we got outside the building, another man was waiting on the porch. I felt that he was CC's partner in crime. He called CC to the side and whispered something in his ear. CC walked away and came to shake my hand.

The man called CC and whispered something to him again. CC yelled, "No man! I told you I'm handling this, OK?"

I started to leave. "You take it easy, CC."

"Do you smoke weed man?" CC called out.

"I have hit a joint or two."

"Well before you go back to Los Angeles, come on back by. We'll smoke together. On me!"

"I may take you up on that CC."

"I'm serious man, on me."

It was daylight, and raining even harder by the time I reached the bus station. I placed my bags in the locker, sat in a chair, and quickly fell asleep.

The rain was still pouring when I woke up. According to the weather reports, Washington had not had as much rain since September 1979. I was wet and cold. It was still a long time before the March was to begin, and I wanted to go home.

I had some money wired to me from California. I had decided that I would rather stay in a hotel than bother my uncle again. I had only met him once and did not know his reasons for not picking me up. I did not want to make him uncomfortable by calling back.

I began calling hotels again. The Days Inn had one room left. I asked them to hold it for me, and I flagged the taxi. The driver asked me about the March and advised me to be careful during my stay in Washington.

"Things are rough here man, all you hear about is killing, killing, killing. You have to watch yourself at all times."

I told him that I would be careful. I was thinking, every city I had visited since I was old enough to leave home had been described the same way.

The streets of Washington DC were now filled with black men. In the lobby of the hotel, I met men from all over the United States and some from other countries. Black men were greeting each other warmly. That was now a feeling of energy and excitement in the air that I had never felt. It felt good to see so many men coming to participate in the March.

I placed my luggage in the room and came back outside to find a restaurant. As the elevator door opened, I heard someone say. "It ain't going to be like them niggers think..."

There were three white men about to get off on that floor. The first one to see me signal the others to be quiet. I looked at them and smiled. There were too many black men around to be concerned.

After I ate, showered, and began to relax. I began to take note of the things I had experienced. There was a rally the night before the March, but I was too tired to attend. I decided to rest so that I could be there when the March was to begin. At 4:00 in the morning.

The day of the March, I got up at 3:00 in the morning, showered and left. I was going to ask some of the men the way to the place where we were to assemble, but I did not have to. All I had to do was follow the crowd. There were lines and lines of black men

MILLION MAN MARCH

on every street headed for the March. It looked as if there were over a million of us there at 4:00.

We passed small groups of white supremist but, seeing the thousands of black men coming from every direction made them leave quickly.

It was cold and dark. I got as close to the front of the crowd as I could, and that was a long way back. I found this seat on a brick wall next to some other men. We were all complaining that sitting on the wall was like sitting on ice, but my feet were hurting too bad to stand. The air was fresh and clean from the rain, but it was dark and cold, and everyone was uncomfortable.

When the organizers finished putting up the speakers, someone put on some music. The first recording was a reggae sound.

it seemed as if the temperature was dropping and some of the men said that it was unusually dark for that time of day.

The song, "what's going on?" by Marvin Gaye began to play and the music seemed to work magically with the crowd. The men started moving to the music, warming up to each other and talking. Men were still coming in from every direction. The lines seem to be endless.

A white man was walking through the crowd. A man standing next to me said. "That white man should be scared as hell walking through here."

"I know I would be, if I were him." Another voice said.

"Nothing but niggers as far as you can see."

"Where are you from man?" I was asked.

"I'm from Los Angeles."

"You came here all the way from LA?"

"Yes."

"I salute you brother. We have got to get together and do something. That little troll, Newt Gingrich, is trying to take us back to slavery."

"Yeah, but we ain't going out like that this time. These white folks plan is going to backfire."

"There are so many niggers here today, the sun is even afraid to come up."

Everyone was now warming up, laughing and talking. There was more politeness and friendliness than I had ever experienced. Everyone joined the conversation. Other conversations started all over the place. You began to hear people yell.

"Detroit in the house!"

"LA in the house!"

"Philly in the house!" The names of cities from all over the United States were being called out.

"Who did you come here with?" Someone asked me.

"I came here alone."

"You came all the way here alone?"

"yes."

"Well, you ain't alone no more. All of your brothers are here today."

"You know man, this thing is great. Can't you feel it?"

Yeah. This thing equals Moses in the Bible, going to the pharaoh telling him to let the people go."

"History is repeating itself. This time we are the children of Israel."

"I used to think we would have to fight a race war. Now something tells me God is going to release plagues on the United States like the people have never seen."

"Yeah, we can look for earthquakes, fires, floods, storms, diseases, everything. They're going to have their hands full fighting Mother Nature. I believe they're going to be hit so hard until they'll never be able to recover."

Isn't it great to know that the Bible stuff is true? That there is a God? That he is on our side?"

"It's funny man. White America is in a position where they're going to have to free us or be destroyed by God. We know they just as stubborn as the pharaoh, so all we have to do is sit back and watch God work."

"They ain't going down easy though. Just like it was in the time of Moses. The more plagues God sends, the eviler they're going to become. We still have to be careful; they are going to take as many of us down with them as they can."

"Did you see those little bottles of water all over the place?"

"Yes, everyone is walking around with those little balls of water they are giving away for free."

"I wouldn't touch one with a 10-foot pole. The whites may have placed it there, it might be poisoned."

"I wouldn't be surprised; they gave the Indians free blankets infected with smallpox."

"For real?"

"Don't put anything past them man. They are blue eyed demons in every sense of the word."

"Did you see how crazy they got when OJ was found not guilty?"

"That, in itself, lets you know we are dealing with crazy people."

"Yes, when the system works for blacks, they want to change it."

"They didn't think this March would be a success, but there are well over a million of us here already."

"Yeah, now the only thing they can do is to lie about how many of us are here." (Some reports did attempt to decrease the number.)

The men continued talking, exchanging stories about discrimination, police brutality, and other racial experiences. The conversations continued until the program began.

It was like a great party where brothers who had been separated by slavery were able to meet each other again. That was so much love until you could feel the presence of God. The speech given by Minister Farrakhan brought tears to our eyes when pointed to a place where brothers had been sold.

Before we left, every man there knew that he had been called there by God. We also knew that each one would have a job to do after the March. My job was to write this book.

www.ingramcontent.com/pod-product-compliance
Lightning Source LLC
LaVergne TN
LVHW061527070526
838199LV00009B/400